Favorite Family Hikes

An Active Family's Guide to Walking in South Carolina

Made possible by underwriting from BMW Manufacturing Co.

Proceeds benefit South Carolina trails and natural resources.

Text by Amanda Capps, Yon Lambert, Ned Cannon and Jennifer Revels.
Design, maps and layout by Susan Jones Ferguson.
Additional Photos by: Yon Lambert, Ned Cannon, Tom Savage.
Edited by Cal Harrison.
Editorial Assistance by Nancy Stone-Collum and Sally Stephens.

Published by: Palmetto Conservation Foundation/PCF Press P.O. Box 1984 Spartanburg, S.C. 29304
www.palmettoconservation.org

10 09 08 07 06 05 04 03 02

Printed in the United States.

Library of Congress Cataloging-in-Publication Data is available.

Important Notc

Please use common sense when using this book! No guidebook can act as a substitute for experience, careful planning, the right equipment and appropriate training. There is inherent danger in all activities described in this book and readers must assume full responsibility for their own actions and safety. Changing or unfavorable conditions in weather, roads, trails and so forth cannot be anticipated by the writers and publisher, but should be considered by outdoor participants. The writers and publisher are not responsible for the safety of users of this guide.

Acknowledgements

This book was made possible by contributions from many people including: Al James, Amber Von Harten, Anne Close, Ben Brooks, Bill Steele, Bob Swanson, Brian Lacey, Chris Eldridge, Chris Reichel, Claire Carey, Dennis Chastain, Frank Stovall, Greg Borgen, James Luken, Jo Anna White, Linda Turner, Martha Bogle, Meg Benko, Melissa LeRoy, Michael Lowe, Mike Dawson, Mike Leslie, Oliver Buckles, Poll Knowland, Rebecca Munnerlyn, Rec Cobb, Scott Stegenga, Tim Cook, Tommy Wyche, Ty Houck, Wendy Coplen and William Hamilton.

Amanda Capps would like to thank all of those work for preservation and conservation in South Carolina; BMW for its generous funding of this publication. She dedicates her work to: musician Harry Bouknight, journalism professor Ronald Farrar, newspaper editor Bob Houston, dad Bennie, late mom Sarah and the rest of her dear family and friends.

30 Favorite Family Hikes

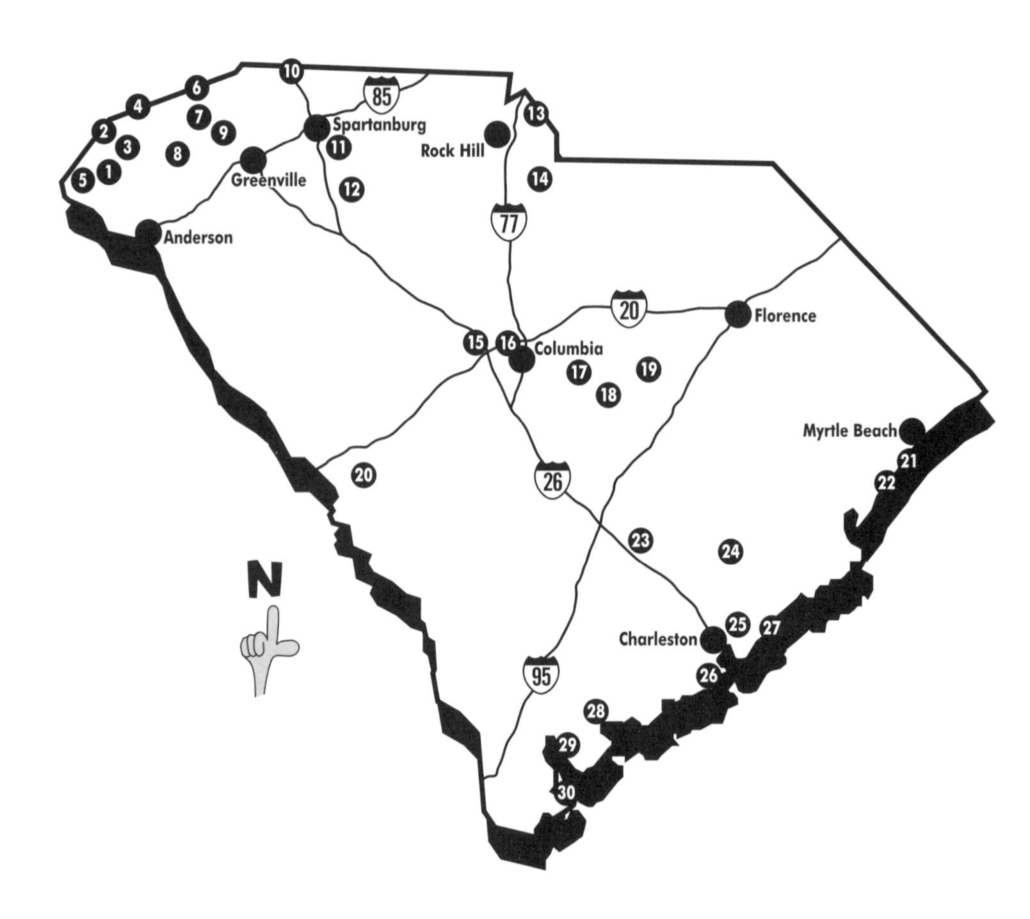

Table of Contents

Foreword by BMW

Whether you are a South Carolina native or a newcomer, such as BMW Manufacturing Co. who has chosen to make the Palmetto State your home, we believe the Favorite Family Hikes book will help you discover some of the state's best places to stretch your legs with your family.

Residents are seeking recreational opportunities in the state's diverse selection of parks, natural areas and urban trails. Colorful Piedmont forests and scenic waterfalls no longer are just the domain of super-fit hikers and bicyclists. Today, it is common to find children, older adults and even entire families traveling to waterfalls and wildlife overlooks in a dense Lowcountry marsh.

The featured trips are designed for families seeking short walks and fun outdoor activities in every part of the state. Make sure you venture beyond your home area to experience each part of the state – the Upstate with its mountains and Paris Mountain State Park, the Midlands with Congaree National Park, the Pee Dee with Cheraw State Park and the Lowcountry with the stunning beaches of Hunting Island.

BMW Manufacturing Co. is proud to partner with the Palmetto Conservation Foundation to promote conservation, preservation and outdoor recreation with this book and by awarding the annual BMW Conservation Award.

It is important to balance environmental quality and economic vitality so that the quality of life can be enhanced for all South Carolinians. BMW Manufacturing is pleased that the proceeds from sales of "Favorite Family Hikes" will be used to support trail and conservation efforts in this state.

Please use this book to explore South Carolina and enjoy it for many years to come.

BMW Manufacturing Co.

Introduction

Compared to South Carolina's children's museums, zoos, aquariums, theaters and amusement parks, a walking guide seems almost old-fashioned. Families are inundated with recreation options and, when we aren't shopping or visiting with relatives, we're running errands. Who really has the time just to walk? What about families with an infant in tow? That was how my wife Diane and I felt for months after the birth of our first child.

After leading very active outdoor lives, our hiking, trail running and climbing took a backseat as we adjusted to a new schedule with different demands. A friend had given us a beautiful Kelty child-carrier backpack that we promised we would employ as soon as our daughter, Sophie, could hold her head upright. But through that first winter and early spring, it hung idly in our garage – a bright-blue monument to our lack of gumption. Sure, we took Sophie on short walks through the neighborhood; she enjoyed the jogging stroller and was a trooper on travels to cities such as Seattle and Portland. But for one reason or another, we never managed to make the leap to walking through the woods, to say nothing of a half-day hike in a mountainous setting.

Then, one spring weekend we grabbed that dusty child carrier, loaded our dogs in the car and drove to a waterfall I had visited many times before. I figured the ease of the hike and my familiarity with the terrain would negate our sad lack of experience at day hiking with a child. We packed the usual necessities – extra diapers, pacifier, plenty of water and snacks – and set out on the trail. We were prepared for the worst, but we learned that day that families and day hiking go hand in hand.

First of all, even as a tiny baby, Sophie was completely at home in the outdoors – not because her parents' "hiking gene" had somehow been passed on to her, but because kids love exploring new environments and being active. Second, and most important, is that many, many other families were also out enjoying the trail. We saw a family with an infant napping in a baby carrier that had been used many times more than ours. Two young parents frolicked in a creek with their three children. A grandmother with four kids – pre-teen to infant – relaxed at an overlook. People of all generations – grandparents, pre-teens and infants – had found this wonderful trail and were enjoying it with their families.

And that started me to thinking ... how many trails in South Carolina are particularly good for family visits? Are there trails all over the state that are well-suited for families in terms of ease of use or nearby amenities that can turn an excuse to hike into a day trip? Many families enjoy camping in South Carolina's state parks and national forests, but what about families that just want to get out for a weekend afternoon and get some physical activity?

At PCF Press, we've already been traveling across the state, hard at work on a guide to some of the best day trips in South Carolina. But expanding that book's scope into our guide to favorite hiking places for families seemed like a great way to improve our book and provide a service to South Carolina families at the same time. Some of these trips, including Congaree National Park, Issaquena Falls and the Awendaw Connector, were already on our list. But after consulting with natural resource professionals from across South Carolina – many of whom were parents, too – we came up with a list of 30 hikes across three regions of the state that were well-suited for families. Inside, you will find trails to mountainside waterfalls and hikes along barrier islands. Some of the hikes are in urban environments, close to important kid considerations such as pizza parlors, while others are set back far from the bustle of modern life.

In truth, the opportunities in South Carolina for short hikes, fun walks, and easy backpacking adventures are almost unlimited. And although this guide is geared toward trips for shorter legs (and attention spans), anyone looking for a less strenuous – but still rewarding – getaway will enjoy this book. As always, let us know what you think!

Yon Lambert
PCF Press, Fall 2004

How to use this Book

Favorite Family Hikes includes 30 hikes in the Mountains, Midlands & Piedmont and Lowcountry. The hikes are numbered 1 through 30 and have been organized for convenient access from the state's major population centers. The terrain varies from mountainside scrambles to boardwalks over swamps. Nearly all of the hikes are less than 5 miles in length and most offer convenient access to amenities.

Each hike includes a text description that outlines what you can expect to see while out on the trail and a standardized list of logistical considerations. The list includes:

Location: The park, forest or private location that has access to the main trailhead of the trail.
Directions: All directions are given from the closest major population center. In as many cases as possible, large cities are referenced, but in some instances we include a reference to a major highway.
Hiking Time: This is the approximate amount of time one could expect to complete the entire trail. In some instances, when we have included a small network of trails or trail that might have opportunities to double-back, we might include a time range such as 30 minutes to 1 hour.
Distance: The linear distance of the trail described, generally as a round trip. We always make sure to say whether the hike is one way or round trip.
Difficulty level: There have been many improvements to the trail-building process in recent years, and trails are more commonly interpreted so hikers can see the expected elevation change, grade and surface type before they leave the trailhead. Nonetheless, the trails included in Favorite Family Hikes were chosen with ease of use in mind. All the trails in this book should be negotiable at least partway by users of all age ranges and physical condition, although some trails do not always have level surfaces. A few of the trails may require scrambling and some make relatively long gradual climbs. Still, assuming adults in average physical condition and walking at normal pace, the trails here are all considered "easy" or "moderate."
Trail surface: All trail descriptions include a note about the surface type. To accommodate users of all abilities, especially those with mobility impairments, senior citizens and children under 10, it is best if trails are firm and level. However, not all trails are built in this manner. By letting users know whether a trail surface is sandy, rocky, crosses tree roots or bridges, we try to make families aware of potential obstacles.
Trail markings: Most trails are signed and marked by blazes on trees or some other directional signage. This section includes information that will help you look for these markings.
Uses: While this guide focuses on great places for families to walk, the locations may also include other activities such as bicycling, water sports or birding. Information about these related activities is often included, but sometimes you may have to supplement this book with more specific information from your destination.
Facilities: Each hike description points out nearby restrooms, water fountains, picnic areas or even camping locations. In some instances, we may point out additional lodging options or locations within the park where snacks or gifts are available.
Best time to visit: Always one season that has the most to offer visitors (i.e. winter).
Dogs: We have contacted each destination to determine whether dogs are allowed and noted where dogs are not allowed. In all cases, dogs must be on a leash.
Fees: The description will note whether or not fees are charged. All fees listed are current through summer 2004.
Hours: When the trail is open to the public.
For more information: Who to contact to get more information about a trail, with telephone number and Web sites.

Preparing for a Family Hike - 10 Essentials

Not all family hikes require extensive preparation or planning. Don't be intimidated by this list. Instead, use it as a general guide and trust your common sense.

1. Dress for the weather but also for comfort, remembering that proper footwear is essential for small hikers as well as adults. Kids can often get by with sneakers instead of hiking boots, but remember to bring an extra pair as well as extra socks. If there is water near the trail, kids will find it and get soaked!

2. Always pack plenty of insect repellant and sunscreen, particularly if you are headed to the coast. Take along first-aid kits and know how to treat common problems such as sunburn, hypothermia, bites, stings and rashes.

3. Teach your children not to drink water from creeks or streams since drinking unpurified water can cause serious problems. Even the clearest and most inviting streams can pose health hazards. Be sure to take enough potable water with you and map nearby sources such as ranger stations along the way.

4. Learn about how to avoid certain plants such as poison ivy. See appendix.

5. Bring rain gear or at least foldable ponchos.

6. If you are planning to enjoy lunch or snacks on the trail, remember to add some extra high-energy snacks such as granola bars, candies or nuts. Kids expend more energy than we do and need to replenish more often.

7. Be sure to stay on designated walkways and trails. Of course it is easy to get lost, but you also are endangering the terrain. U.S. Geological Survey topographic maps are useful and can be purchased from outdoor supply shops. State parks and most sites within this book have maps available free of charge. Always stay off private property, unless it is part of a designated trail.

8. Bring baby wipes, since little hands often find dirty bugs, tree sap and sand, sand, sand!
Leave a copy of your hiking route with a forest ranger or wildlife officer. Many sites in the book require registration.

9. Be sure you are familiar with the types of wildlife you may encounter out on the trail. A minimal amount of homework will help you identify certain species and know why they are protected - or to be avoided!

10. If you are a novice, do not overestimate your abilities - or underestimate the weather. Knowledge is the first step to a safe and enjoyable vacation.

Visitors' Etiquette – Leave No Trace

Remember that you are a guest in the great outdoors. "Pack out what you pack in" is a common way of saying that you should leave the area as undisturbed as possible. Litter is unfortunately a common problem. Also, do not remove anything from preserved sites. Do not chop down trees for firewood, pick wild plants and flowers or disturb wildlife. Unlike more developed recreational areas, protected sites were not built primarily for human consumption and entertainment. Help preserve them and leave our beautiful natural resources and heritage for future generations.

Mountains

Text by Amanda Capps

The Mountains region – which for purposes of this book includes portions of Oconee, Pickens, Greenville and Spartanburg counties north of Interstate 85 – is replete with opportunities for outdoor family adventures. Here, cascading waterfalls, crystal blue lakes, exotic vegetation and plenty of fresh mountain air make this area a favorite among South Carolina's many natural attractions. The Cherokee Foothills Scenic Highway, which connects many of the sites found in this book, was named one of the most scenic drives in America by *Reader's Digest's Illustrated Reference Book.* From this highway families can access many of the hikes detailed here. Table Rock State Park and the Cherokee Foothills Visitor's Center provide a fine introduction to the entire area, but specifically for sites in Oconee, Pickens and Greenville Counties. Table Rock is known for its accommodating meeting facilities. With a multi-purpose recreation center, two picnic shelters and a banquet capacity for 175 guests, it is a popular destination for corporate retreats and family reunions. However, legend has it that the "Great Spirit" of the Cherokee Indians was the first to dine upon the eponymous flat rock.

Greenville County – the state's most populous county – is the metropolitan hub of the Upstate. Farther west and surrounded by lakes and rivers, Oconee County is also home to the largest concentration of waterfalls in South Carolina. Visitors from all over travel here to enjoy the magnificent and remarkably dissimilar cascades. The county's premiere water-based attraction is the Chattooga River, which is also one of the most revered whitewater destinations in the Southeast. The Chattooga was the first river east of the Mississippi to receive the designation as a "Wild and Scenic River." The corridor that parallels the river is protected, so visitors can enjoy nearly 50 miles of undeveloped scenery as they shoot past the Sumter National Forest. The water drops 2,500 feet as it rushes toward the backwaters of Tugaloo Lake.

Finally, Spartanburg County mixes Revolutionary War battlefields and tiny mill villages for one of the state's most historic areas. Spartanburg is one of the few areas that offer family-oriented hikes in both the Mountains and Midlands sections. In the county's northern reaches, spacious equestrian farms give way to steep mountains in little-known areas such as the Nature Conservancy's Blue Wall Preserve or the Foothills Equestrian Nature Center. Families have a diverse number of places to enjoy.

Note! *While many family-friendly opportunities are available throughout the Mountains region, it is important to remember that we focused on just a few areas close to the trails in this book. Make sure that you do plenty of exploring too!*

Detours *Whatever destination you are visiting in Oconee, Greenville, Pickens or Spartanburg counties, rest assured there are many places off the beaten path that can add some excellent local color to your trip. Here are some of the most family-oriented locations in this region:*

Oconee & Anderson Counties: *For hikes #1-5: Oconee Connector, Licklog & Pigpen Falls, Issaqueena Falls, Lower Whitewater Falls and Chau Ram County Park*

In the Mountain Rest area, children always enjoy watching the rainbow trout racing through the aquatic corridors of the Walhalla State Fish Hatchery. Located approximately eight miles north of Oconee State Park, the hatchery stocks hundreds of thousands of trout in South Carolina waters every year to offset heavy fishing and low nutrient levels in area waters. The Sumter National Forest Chattooga Picnic Area is also close to the hatchery.

Near Walhalla, the Oconee Station State Historic Site marks the oldest building in the county, a fieldstone structure thought to be more than 240 years old. Oconee Station served as a military outpost when conflict arose between settlers and Indians. Just outside the historic site, Station Cove Falls cascades over 60 feet of wide, rocky steps. Mayapple, pink lady slipper and orchids are a few of the wildflowers that bloom near the falls. The falls are accessible from the Oconee Connector of the Palmetto Trail (hike #1). To reach the falls from Walhalla, drive 3.5 miles north on SC 183 and take a left onto SC 11. Follow SC 11 for 1.5 miles and take a left onto Oconee Station Road. The trailhead is approximately 0.3 miles past the historic site, and the hike to the falls is 0.5 miles.

On the banks of Lake Keowee near Seneca, Duke Power's World of Energy makes the connection between electricity and the elements that generate it. Self-guided tours are free of charge, and children will appreciate educational computer games. The World of Energy is located at the Keowee-Toxaway Center just off SC 183.

In Clemson, the T. Ed Garrison Arena is a well-known spot for rodeo fans. Originally built to promote the livestock industry, the venue hosts a wide variety of trade shows, concerts and other events. Livestock shows and sales are held at the arena, which is also equipped with barns and milking operations. Visitors can attend a rodeo or learn to compete in one. Several schools teach the finer points of riding, roping and more throughout the year. The arena is located off I-85 (Exit 19B toward Clemson on US 76).

Anderson's Freedom Weekend Aloft is one of South Carolina's most unique and celebrated festivals. Typically held on Memorial Day Weekend, this event is centered on the arrival of a vivid bouquet of hot air balloons. Freedom Weekend is the nation's second-largest hot air balloon event. Held at the Anderson Sports and Entertainment Center, the festival includes an air show, parasailors, amusement park rides, kids' activities and national recording artists. Entertainers in 2003 ranged from Tracy Lawrence to David Lee Roth. The nearby Anderson County Arts Center on North Main Street features local, regional and national artists, as well as traveling exhibits. Visitors can enjoy the pottery gallery or the Annual Juried Show, which draws hundreds of artists from across the Southeast.

Pickens County: *For hikes #6-8: Town Creek Trail, Blue Ridge Electric CoOp Passage of the Palmetto Trail, Twin Falls*

In the Pickens County area, families will find plenty of good food and souvenirs at Aunt Sue's Country Corner, located two miles east of Table Rock State Park on SC 11. The corner is actually a village of several shops including The Rock House, which offers gem mining. The Wood House features carvings by local artists, and The Ice Cream House offers homemade cones, cobblers and fudge.

Hagood Mill - a circa-1845 gristmill - is the only one in the state operating with its original wheel components. Public demonstrations are offered on the third Saturday of each month from 9 a.m. to 4 p.m. and by appointment. Take home an edible token of South Carolina's history in the form of cornmeal or grits. Visitors of all ages may also enjoy living history presentations, the Old Bear Blacksmith Shop, the Mill Race Nature Trail and the Cherokee Home Site. Pickens County's Upcountry Folklife Festival and Old Time Fiddlin' Convention are held at Hagood in September. To find the mill from Pickens, drive north on US 178 for three miles to Hagood Mill Road and follow the signs.

If you're an angler looking for the best fishing spots, try Fish, Inc., which offers expeditions on Lake Jocassee aboard a 32-foot pontoon. Day trips and overnight excursions are available. The tours include top fishing spots, as well as sightseeing near area waterfalls. Additional services include shuttle service to and from the Foothills Trail, refreshments, steak dinners and transportation for scuba divers.

Budding young collectors will be thrilled by one of the largest gem collections in the Southeast at Bob Campbell Geology Museum. Meteorites and fossils provide glimpses of history and the world beyond ours, while minerals are best viewed under the ultraviolet light of the museum's darkroom. Free group tours are available. While visiting this site, remind children to look for feldspar, biotite, quartz and amphiobole - all components of Table Rock. The museum is on the Clemson University campus, 11 miles southwest of Pickens.

In Liberty, Ferne's Miniatures/Dollhouse Museum & Shop, located at 510 Flat Rock Road, boasts more than 700 dolls along with antique and modern houses and accessories. Some items are for sale. The facility is open by appointment only and requests that all visitors be at least 10 years old.

Greenville & Spartanburg Counties: *(For hikes #9-10: Lake Placid and Blue Wall Passage of the Palmetto Trail)*

Greenville is the main metropolitan neighbor to the mountains region. Larger and more cosmopolitan than its Upstate cousins, Greenville has multiple shopping malls, movie theaters and restaurants that range from popular chains to eclectic downtown eateries. Couples and single adults may opt for the acclaimed Peace Center for the Performing Arts, an extensive collection of Andrew Wyeth watercolors at the Greenville County Museum of Art or a night's stay at the recently restored Westin Poinsett Hotel downtown. Young people will enjoy the Greenville Zoo and the nature trails of Reedy River Falls Historic Park (downtown). For a more educational experience, try the Roper Mountain Science Center, which has the largest planetarium in South Carolina and the seventh-largest telescope in the country.

In Spartanburg, the BMW Manufacturing Co. off Interstate 85 is a testament to the Upstate's economic strength and progressive growth patterns. Admission to the family-friendly BMW Zentrum is free, and tours of the plant are available for a small fee (by reservation only). Cars on display in the Zentrum span more than 60 years of BMW innovation and style. But the technology extends far beyond automobiles. Aircraft engines, motorcycles and concept cars are also part of the story. For art lovers, the "art car collection" features BMWs with paint schemes designed by Warhol, Lichtenstein and Calder. Those who favor function over form will want to see the virtual factory tour. The Zentrum expresses all of BMW's talents and passions – including the company's commitment to the environment. The facility is just off I-85 (Exit 60) on the outskirts of Spartanburg.

Spartanburg

In Spartanburg – although it's not exactly white-linen dining – visitors need to visit the (in)famous Beacon Drive-in (585 Reidville Road), which serves some of the most famous burgers in the business. The Beacon's chaotic splendor and giant chili cheeseburgers were even featured on national television by legendary journalist Charles Kuralt. First-time visitors should be warned that customers are expected to be ready to order when they approach the counter. Insults from the staff are part of the charm.

A place not far from I-85 and I-26 has become a haven for retired "celebrities." Anyone vacationing with children will want to detour to a place where famous faces abound – Hollywild Animal Park. Dozens of critters that have appeared on television and in movies live in the park, along with 500 of their closest friends. The word "zoo" is never used to describe the park where inhabitants are free to roam within large natural spaces. Visitors can feed and pet some of the animals. You can even spot hidden newborns on a bus tour of the 70-acre park. Because they were raised to be in the spotlight, most of the animals are comfortable around guests. Hollywild has one of the largest exotic animal collections in this part of the country. To get to the park, take Exit 15 off I-26 and travel approximately six miles on SC 292.

Located just off I-85, the Gaffney area is a necessary stop on a tour of U.S. history. Cowpens National Battlefield commemorates the day Daniel Morgan led unwavering Continental soldiers to victory over British forces. Wild cherry and dogwood trees set the tone as visitors take an easy 1.2-mlle stroll past 10 exhibit areas. A little farther north, Kings Mountain National Military Park marks another poignant victory. The Oct. 7, 1780, Kings Mountain battle demolished a significant portion of Gen. Cornwallis' army and prevented the British from advancing into North Carolina. Both sites stage re-enactments, but visitors are welcome to view the grounds, along with fascinating multimedia presentations year-round. Other historic sites include the old quarry at Limestone College, which provided the stone that represents South Carolina in the Washington Monument. Limestone College was founded in 1845 and has several buildings on the National Register of Historic Places. Every July, Gaffney welcomes thousands to its Peach Festival, which first drew national attention in 1978 with the world's largest peach pie. Since then, top entertainers such as Reba McIntyre and George Straight have graced the stage every summer. Anytime peaches are in season, travelers can stop by one of several area retailers for peach jam or cider. You'll know you're near Gaffney when you see the Peachoid, a 1 million gallon water tank shaped like the famous fruit.

For more information

Anderson County Arts Center (864) 224-8811

Bob Campbell Geology Museum (864) 656-4600

Cowpens National Battlefield (864) 461-2828

Duke Power's World of Energy (800) 777-1004

Ferne's Miniature Dollhouse Museum and Shop (864) 843-2486

Freedom Weekend Aloft (864) 232-3700

Glenn Springs Historic District (864) 596-3501

Greater Greenville Chamber of Commerce (864) 242-1050

Greater Pickens Chamber of Commerce (864) 878-3258

Hagood Mill (864) 898-5963

Hollywild (864) 472-2038 or (877) Hollywild

Kings Mountain National Battlefield (864) 936-7921

Kings Mountain State Park (803) 222-3209

Nantahala Outdoor Center (800) 232-7238

Oconee State Park (864) 638-5353

Oconee Station State Historic Site (864) 638-0079

Roper Mountain Science Center (864) 281-1188

Peach Festival (864) 489-5716

Table Rock State Park (864) 878-9813

The Zentrum (888) Tour-BMW

USDA Forest Service (for Chattooga River information) (864) 638-9568

Walhalla State Fish Hatchery (864) 638-2866

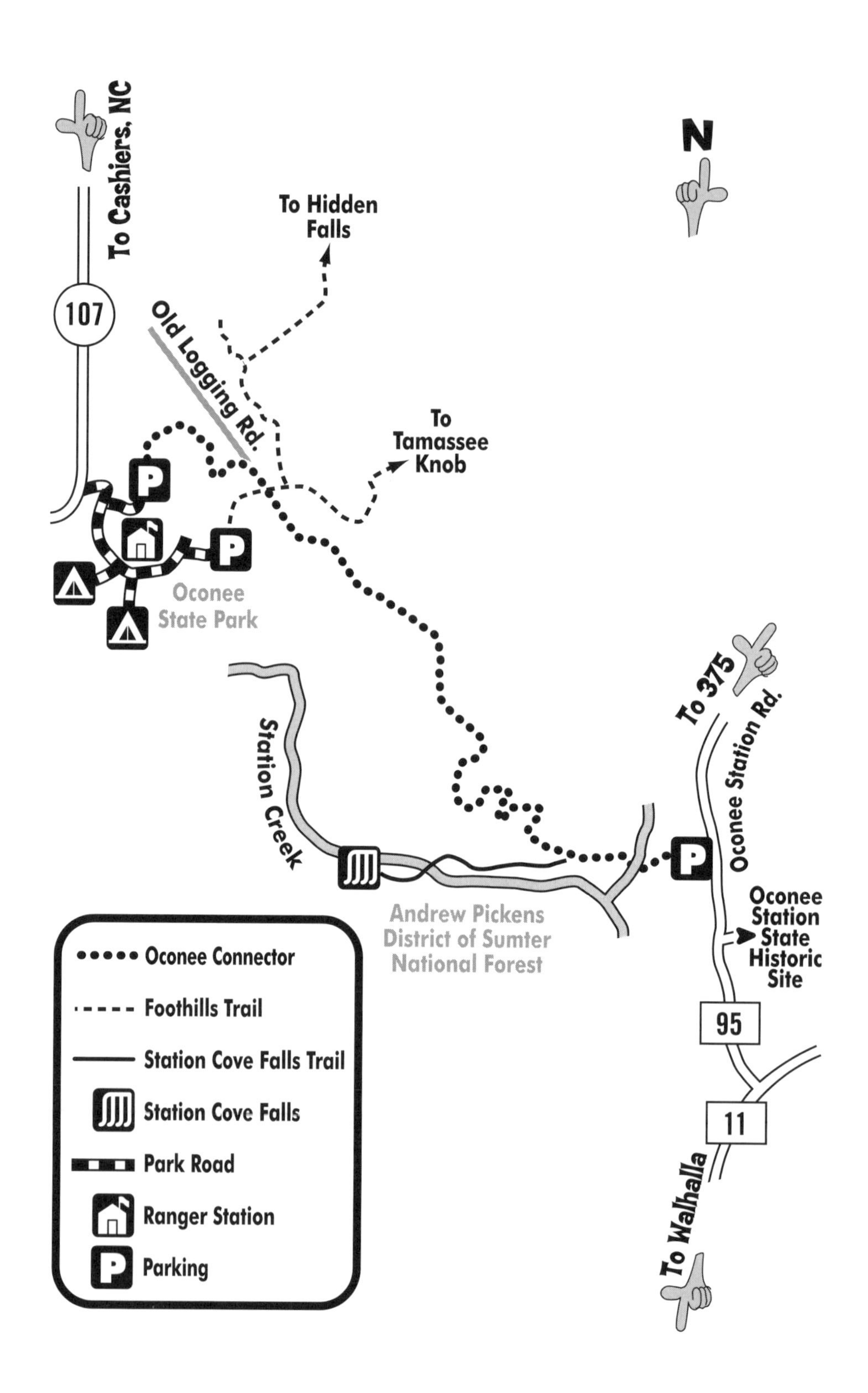
To Cashiers, NC
107
N
To Hidden Falls
Old Logging Rd.
To Tamassee Knob
Oconee State Park
Station Creek
To 375
Oconee Station Rd.
Andrew Pickens District of Sumter National Forest
Oconee Station State Historic Site
95
11
To Walhalla
Oconee Connector
Foothills Trail
Station Cove Falls Trail
Station Cove Falls
Park Road
Ranger Station
Parking

Oconee Connector of the Palmetto Trail

Location: Oconee State Park (Oconee County)
Directions: From Walhalla, drive west on SC 28 for 8.4 miles and bear right (north) onto SC 107. Drive another 2.5 miles to the entrance of Oconee State Park on the right. After the Fee Station turn right and follow signs to the old archery range, which is now the northern terminus for the Palmetto Trail.
Hiking Time: Approximately 3 hours (one way)
Distance: 6.8 miles (round trip)
Difficulty level: Moderate (the trail is rated most difficult on a mountain bike.)
Trail surface: The trail is a natural surface near Oconee State Park and joins a woods road (recently surfaced with crushed stone) as it descends toward Oconee Station.
Trail markings: Kiosk at trailhead, yellow blazes on the Palmetto Trail.
Uses: Hiking, mountain biking, birding
Facilities: Drinking water, restrooms and a drink machine are available at the park office.
Best time to visit: Fall and early spring are favorites. The wildflowers near Station Cove Falls are tremendous in the spring.
Dogs: Yes, on a leash.
Fees: $2 per person for adults; $1.50 for seniors; free for those 15 & younger.
Hours: The park is open 7 a.m. to 7 p.m. Sunday to Thursday; 7 a.m. to 9 p.m., Friday and Saturday. Closing hours extended during Daylight Savings Time.
For more information: Oconee State Park
624 State Park Road
Mountain Rest, SC 29644
(864) 638-5353
www.discoversouthcarolina.com

Family Perk

Of all mountain-region state parks, Oconee may have the most comfortable amenities for family trips. If you plan to stay here overnight, you must book a cabin well in advance of your stay!

Photo courtesy PCF.

Oconee State Park blends the rugged characteristics of a national forest with amenities such as a park store, playground, carpet golf, family campground and rental cabins. For families traveling with both committed outdoorsmen and casual campers, Oconee is a perfect vacation venue. A highlight of this diverse park is the new 3.2-mile (one way) Oconee Connector of the Palmetto Trail, which meanders from the park along a scenic old roadbed and eventually descends into Station Cove, the site of a popular 60-foot waterfall. The trail - which is a great length for a half-day family hike - is the first bicycle and pedestrian connection between Oconee State Park and nearby Oconee Station State Historic Site, formerly accessible only by a 30-minute drive.

The U.S. Forest Service, Dept. of Parks, Recreation and Tourism, National Forest Foundation and the Palmetto Conservation Foundation worked together to build the Oconee Connector, an idea that has been around for a more than a decade. The trail is moderate in difficulty (unless you are on a mountain bike, in which case it is most difficult) although the 1,000-foot change in elevation from the bottom of Station Cove to the ridgeline is challenging. It should still not pose problems to a fit 10-year-old. Starting from Oconee State Park, the trail passes the old archery range and a stone dam from the days of the Civilian Conservation Corps before meandering over a bridge and into the woods. In a short distance, the trail emerges at an old forest service road, which it follows southeast. The wide road soon pinches down as it becomes the old Station Mountain Road, which may have been an Indian trading path during the late 18th century when Oconee Station was established as a garrison to help guard against Cherokee raids and illegal trading.

The trail follows the road on a gradual descent to the southeast with fantastic views during winter and early spring. It eventually veers right (due south) to begin a steeper descent down a ridge above Station Cove, which is one of the richest wildflower areas in the entire state. During the spring wildflower period, visitors can see Pink Ladies' Slippers, trillium, iris and many more. Please stay on the trail. At the bottom of this section, the Oconee Connector joins the existing Station Cove Falls Trail at a wooden stile. If you are on a mountain bike, dismount and park your bike. Hiking only is allowed on the 0.25-mile trail to the fantastic 60-foot waterfall. Backtrack to return to Oconee State Park.

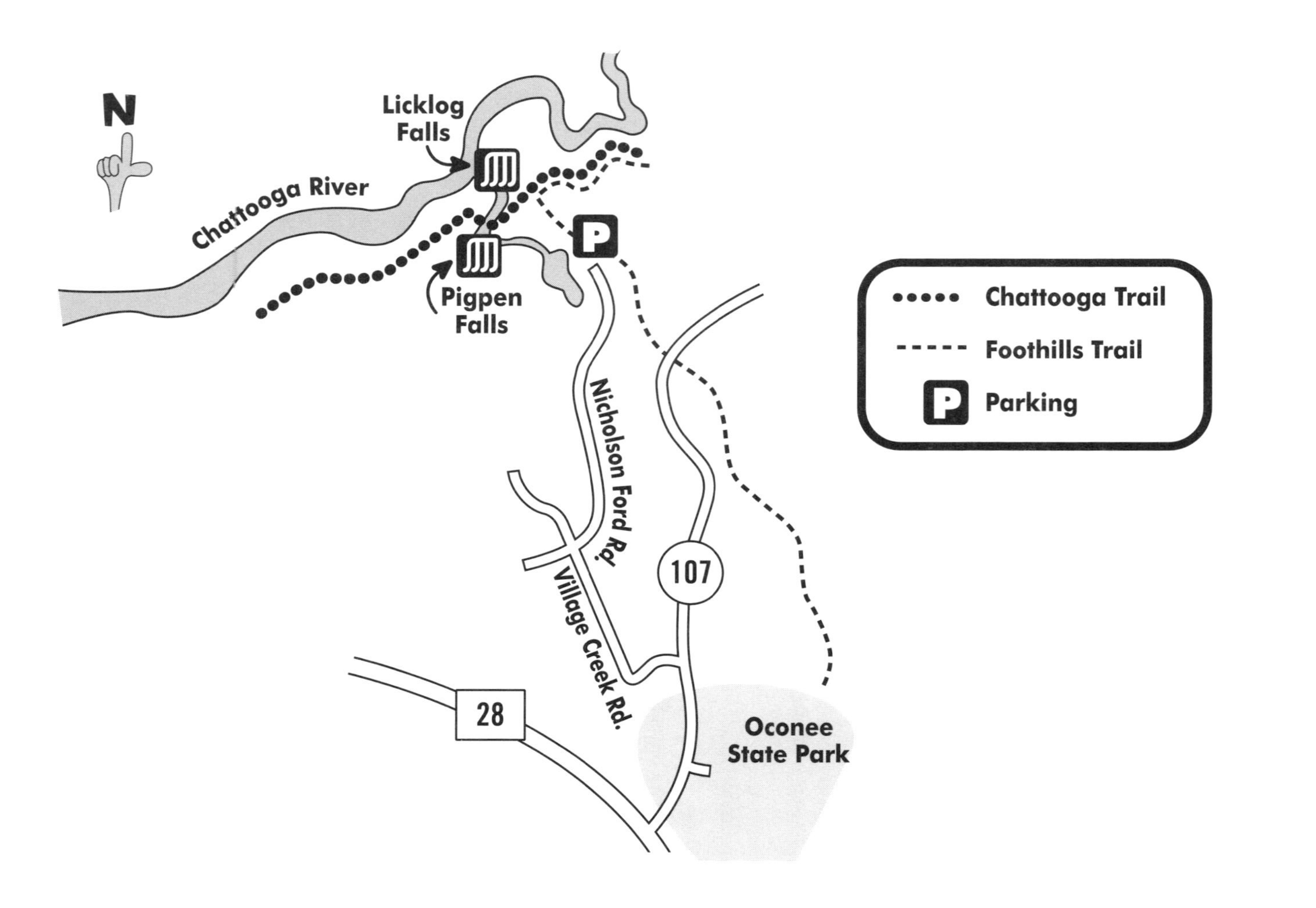

N
Licklog
Falls
Chattooga River
Pigpen
Falls
P
Chattooga Trail
Foothills Trail
P
Parking
Nicholson Ford Rd.
107
Village Creek Rd.
28
Oconee
State Park

Licklog & Pigpen Falls

Location: Sumter National Forest (Oconee County)
Directions: From Walhalla, drive northwest on SC 28 for 8.4 miles and bear right (north) onto SC 107. Drive 3.1 miles and turn left (west) onto Village Creek Road, just past the entrance to Oconee State Park. Drive 1.7 miles and turn right onto Nicholson Ford Road (FS 775), which is gravel. Drive 2.2 miles to a parking area on the right. Park and access the Foothills Trail at the northwest corner of the lot. Hike west on the Foothills Trail (white blaze) for .5 mile and turn left onto the Chattooga Trail. Hike about 0.5-mile to Pigpen Falls. Cross the footbridge and continue for 0.2 mile on the Chattooga Trail and the first level of Licklog Falls will be to the right of the trail. The second level is approximately 50 yards downstream of the first.
Hiking Time: Approximately 30 minutes
Distance: 0.9-mile (one way)
Difficulty level: Easy
Trail surface: Natural trail surface
Trail markings: The trail is marked and blazed as part of the Foothills Trail (white blaze) and Chattooga Trail.
Uses: Hiking
Facilities: A primitive campsite (no water or utilities) is available near the trailhead
Best time to visit: Summer is ideal as the two falls offer small pools for swimming.
Dogs: Yes, on a leash.
Fees: None
Hours: Open 24 hours a day.
For More Information:
Andrew Pickens Ranger District
112 Andrew Pickens Circle
Mountain Rest, SC 29664.
(864) 638-9568
www.fs.fed.us/r8/fms/

Family Perk

Oconee County is the largest apple producing county in South Carolina and the annual Apple Festival, which takes place mid-September, has children's activities, a float on the Chattooga River and a rodeo.

Photo by Ned Cannon.

For most families the hallowed words "two-for-one" demand attention no matter what the circumstances. The easy 0.9-mile hike to Licklog and Pigpen Falls is no exception, as visitors can enjoy two delightful waterfalls on one short, 30-minute hike that even takes you to a section of the Chattooga River. Before we begin the description to this hike, let's be clear: These waterfalls are not a great destination for their sheer splendor alone. In truth, both the 25-foot Licklog and Pigpen Falls are not the most photogenic waterfalls in the area. But since both falls feature deep, sandy-bottomed swimming holes where children can splash and play in a unique natural environment, it is an excellent hike for families.

Pigpen Falls - which is about 0.5-mile from the trailhead - is really two long, divided veils that plunge into an excellent wading pool. The waterfall has a second tier (both tiers are drops of about 12 feet) but it is difficult to see. After playing for a while at the base of this waterfall, you can continue on to Licklog Falls by following the Chattooga Trail across a wooden footbridge over Lick Log Creek. The trail shortly passes the upper tier of this waterfall (families should not take the side path down to the base as it can be slick and dangerous) and soon makes a sharp left along the banks of the Chattooga River. There is a small, unmarked path here down to the base of the falls.

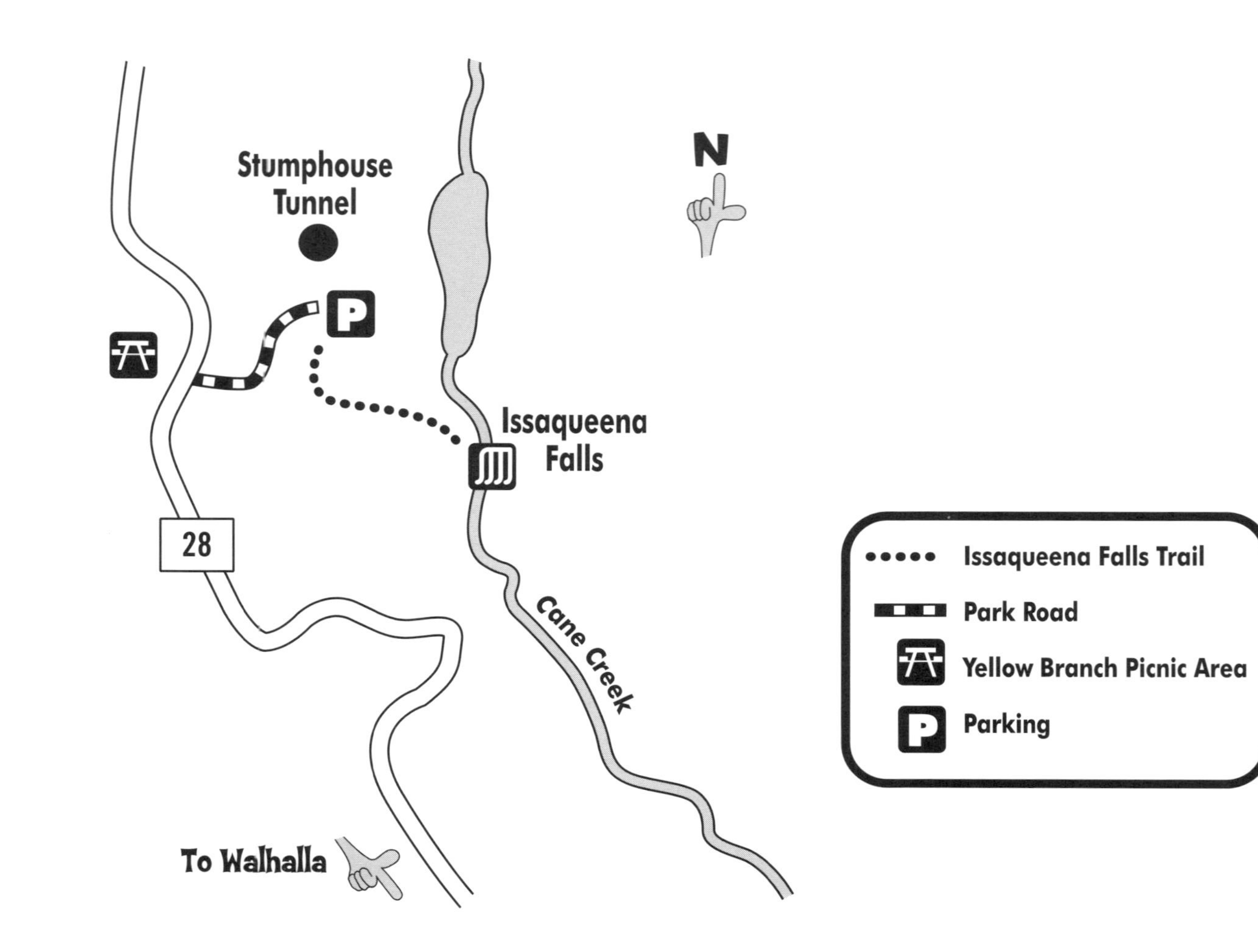

Stumphouse Tunnel
N
Issaqueena Falls
28
Cane Creek
To Walhalla
Issaqueena Falls Trail
Park Road
Yellow Branch Picnic Area
Parking

Issaqueena Falls

Location: Stumphouse Tunnel Picnic Area (Oconee County)
Directions: From Walhalla drive west on SC 28 for 6.9 miles and turn right into Stumphouse Tunnel Park. Pass through the gate and follow the road to the parking lot and picnic area on the right. Park and walk across the footbridge on the west side of the parking lot. From here a path curving to the right side of the falls is apparent. A new viewing deck gives a fine view of the falls and its boulder-strewn creek course through the deeply incised valley below.
Hiking Time: Approximately 30 minutes (one way)
Distance: 0.2 mile
Difficulty level: Easy
Trail surface: Natural trail surface; the short hike to the viewing deck is easy for visitors of all ages and abilities. Adventurous and physically able visitors may opt for the difficult, steep hike down to the falls.
Trail markings: The short hike to the viewing deck is well marked; the trail down to the falls is not marked.
Uses: Hiking
Facilities: Portable toilet, a small shelter with picnic tables
Best time to visit: The viewing deck provides an excellent view in the fall as the leaves begin to change.
Dogs: Yes, on a leash.
Fees: None
Hours: Open daily 10 a.m. to 5 p.m.
For more information:
Walhalla City Hall
206 N. Church St.
Walhalla, SC 29691
(864) 638-4343

Family Perk

In summer, Stumphouse Tunnel is a must-visit location for adventurous children! Be sure to bring headlamps or flashlights and explore deep into the dark tunnel. Just past the old airshaft, you'll even see hundreds of brown bats!

Photo by Ned Cannon.

Though short, the 30-minute hike to the Issaqueena Falls overlook is a fabulous cross section of Oconee County's lush environment. The 100-foot cascading waterfall is sure to please even the toughest critic. The hike is an excellent excursion for families, and it's loaded with local lore and history. Children will love hearing the story of the Indian Princess Issaqueena or visiting the nearby Civil War-era Stumphouse Tunnel.

The falls' name is supposedly derived from a Choctaw princess. Issaqueena, as the story goes, fell in love with an English trader. This love didn't sit too well with the local chief and Issaqueena was ordered to renounce her love. Upon refusing to do this, the princess was placed in captivity and shunned by her people. Issaqueena then learned of a plan to attack the nearby English colony and kill the settlers. Risking her life, she escaped from her village to warn the colony, pursued closely by an angry group of her people. Once at the falls Issaqueena hid underneath a ledge to evade the approaching search party. The furious Indians approached the falls, and believing Issaqueena had jumped over the edge, turned back. As the legend goes Issaqueena eventually reached the colony in time to warn the settlers and ended up marrying the Englishman.

Remember that the hike to the falls overlook is the only route recommended to families. Some visitors opt for a steep, slick path to the base of the waterfall, but this is not a good place for children.

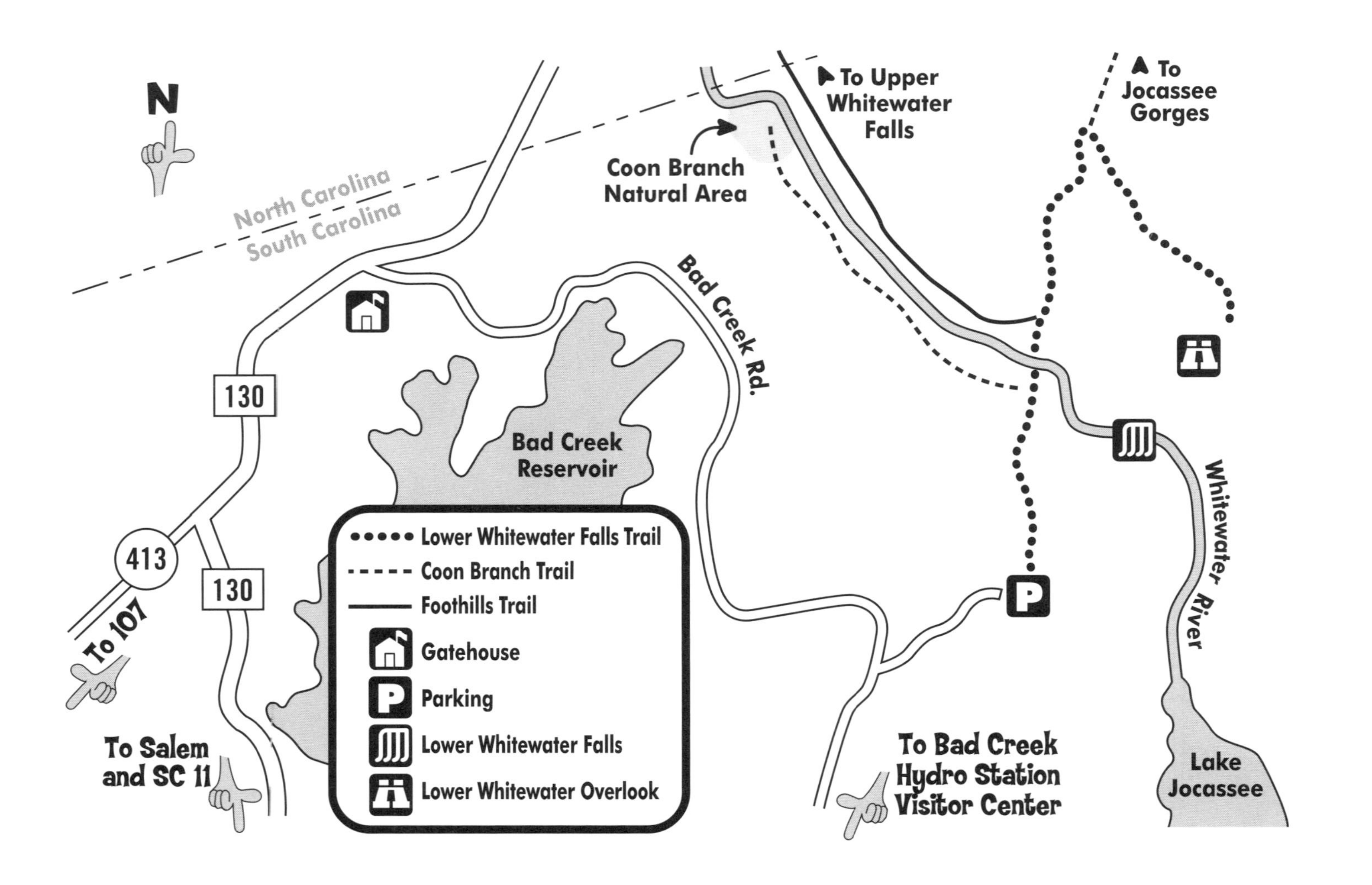

N
North Carolina
South Carolina
To Upper Whitewater Falls
To Jocassee Gorges
Coon Branch Natural Area
Bad Creek Rd.
Bad Creek Reservoir
130
130
413
To 107
To Salem and SC 11
Lower Whitewater Falls Trail
Coon Branch Trail
Foothills Trail
Gatehouse
Parking
Lower Whitewater Falls
Lower Whitewater Overlook
To Bad Creek Hydro Station Visitor Center
Whitewater River
Lake Jocassee

Lower Whitewater Falls

Location: Duke Power Bad Creek Hydroelectric Station (Oconee County)
Directions: From Walhalla, drive north on SC 11 (Cherokee Foothills Scenic Highway) for 14 miles and turn left onto SC 130. Drive north on SC 130 for 10.5 miles and turn right (east) at the entrance to Duke Power's Bad Creek Hydroelectric Station. Pass through the automatic gate. Drive approximately 2 miles to the parking area for the Foothills Trail/Whitewater River.
Hiking Time: 45 minutes to 1 hour (one way)
Distance: 2 miles
Difficulty level: Moderate
Trail surface: Natural trail surface and some gravel roads. The trail crosses one large stream.
Trail markings: Blue trail blazes
Uses: Hiking
Facilities: Restrooms, telephone
Best time to visit: Fall
Dogs: Yes, on a leash.
Fees: None.
Hours: Dawn to dusk.
For more information:
Duke Power World of Energy Visitor's Center
7812 Rochester Highway
Seneca, SC 29678
(800) 777-1004
www.dukepower.com

Family Perk

It's great fun to combine a trip to Lower Whitewater Falls with a stopover at Duke Power's World of Energy, which includes free admission to interactive activities about how energy is created.

Photo courtesy PCF.

A moderate 45-minute hike will seem well worth your time upon seeing the dramatic Lower Whitewater Falls in Oconee County. The falls have been inspiring trekkers, poets, and artists alike for nearly two centuries. In 1847, South Carolina novelist William Gilmore Simms wrote in his travel journal, "There is hardly anything more beautiful in all the country." Who are we to argue?

These days, visitors can enjoy the falls from a viewing platform built in 1991 by the combined efforts of local public and private organizations. While obviously improving the view, the platform also shaves nearly 2 hours off the former hike required for a look at the falls. Although it has no single fall to match its taller (and far more popular) sister in North Carolina, Lower Whitewater Falls rushes down a gorge with tremendous verve, creating a view that is sure to stir your soul. This hike is a must for all families.

From the trailhead at the far end of the parking area, follow the blue blazes of the Lower Whitewater Falls overlook spur. At 0.6 mile the spur will cross over the Whitewater River on a 60-foot steel bridge. Turn right (northeast). At this point the trail runs concurrently with the Jocassee Gorges Segment of the Foothills Trail bound for Laurel Valley. (The Foothills Trail is marked with white blazes.) When the trail intersects a gravel road, follow the gravel road briefly (about 200 yards) and then resume your hike on the trail. A blue blaze and an arrow sign on the right point the way. Continue to the overlook.

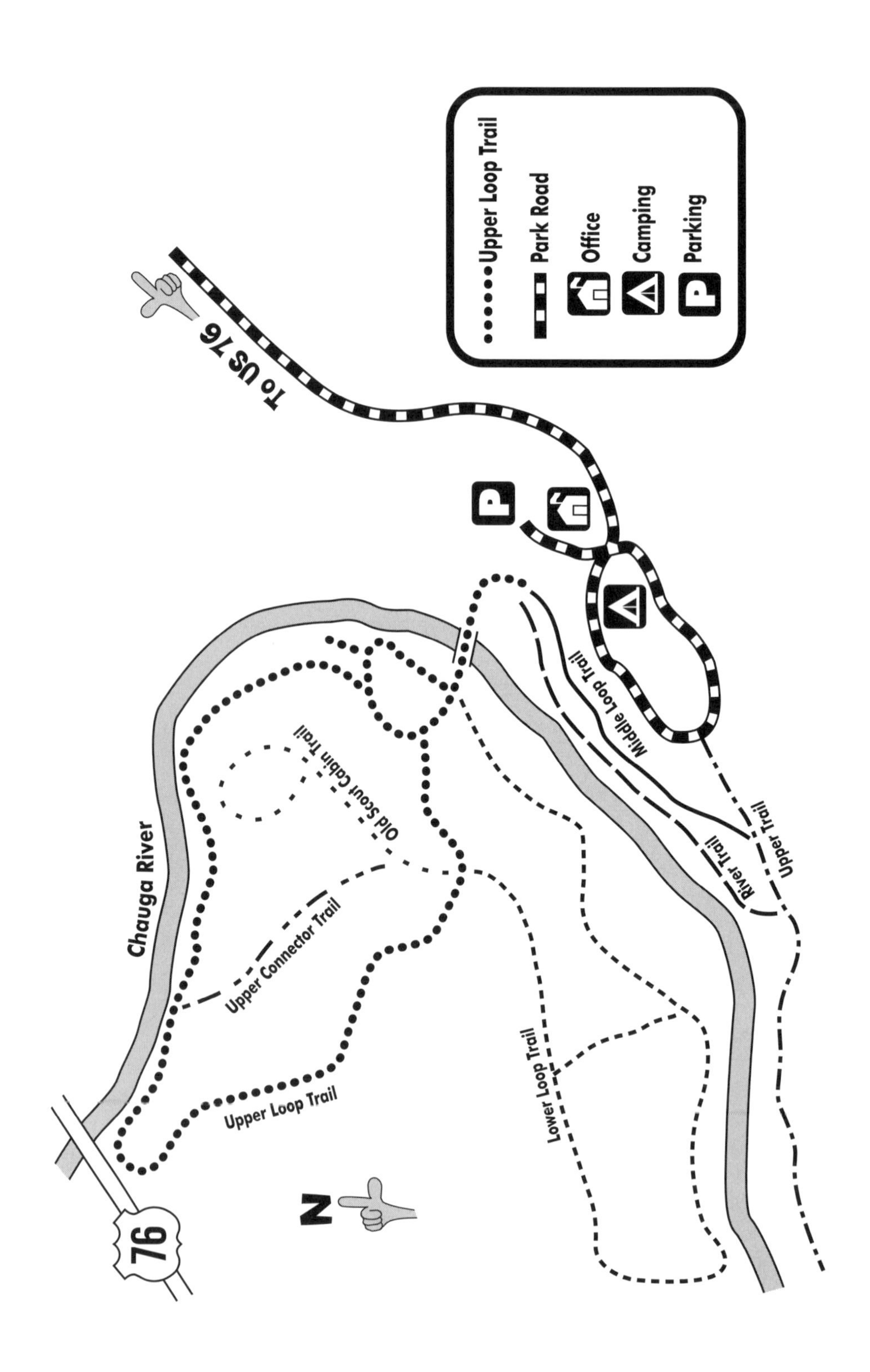
Upper Loop Trail
Park Road
Office
Camping
Parking
To US 76
Chauga River
Middle Loop Trail
Old Scout Cabin Trail
Upper Connector Trail
Upper Loop Trail
Lower Loop Trail
River Trail
Upper Trail
N
76

Chau Ram County Park

Location: Chau Ram County Park (Oconee County)
Directions: From Westminster, drive west on US 76. Keep right at the fork with US 123 and drive another 2.5 miles. Turn left onto Chau Ram Park Road and continue to the park entrance at the end of the road. You can park on the right, or follow the park road loop to the lower-level parking area.
Hiking Time: 30 minutes to 2 hours
Distance: 4 miles of interconnecting trails
Difficulty level: Easy to moderate
Trail surface: Natural surface trails along rolling/rugged terrain. These trails are not suitable for people with mobility impairments.
Trail markings: The trails are blazed and maps are available online and in the park office.
Uses: Hiking, fishing, kayaking, rafting, swimming, camping and picnicking
Facilities: Restrooms, drinking water, drink machines and picnic shelters are located near the park office.
Best time to visit: Summer is ideal at this riverside park.
Dogs: Yes, on a leash.
Fees: None
Hours: Open 7 a.m. to dusk
For more information:
Oconee County Parks, Recreation and Tourism
1220 Chau Ram Park Rd.
Westminster, SC 29693
864) 647-9286
www.oconeesc.com/parks/

Family Perk

Book a rafting trip while visiting this park (NOC: (800) 232-7238) Many families use this park as a base when rafting on the nearby Chattooga River.

Photo by Ned Cannon.

Tucked away at the end of a residential road, Chau Ram Park is known as Oconee County's "best kept secret" and after a visit families will see why it's a secret worth keeping. For adventurous families the nearly 4 miles of interconnecting Chau Ram Park Trails might be the reason. A bouncy walk across one of the Upstate's only suspension bridges leads you to the easy/moderate trails that wind along the picturesque hillsides, ridges, and rocky banks of the Chauga River. Whether you're using the trails to reach a good swimming location or just out enjoying the sanctity of nature your family will have no problems following these easily navigable trails. And if that doesn't satisfy your adventure craving families can also choose from a number of activities including tubing, kayaking and fishing, although no rental facilities are onsite.

For families that aren't so adventure-hungry Chau Ram offers a number of locations for simply lounging and enjoying the view. Picnic facilities are located riverside for nearly a quarter mile stretch and scattered throughout the rest of the park; even on crowded days your family will have no problem staking out a little piece of the park to call your own.

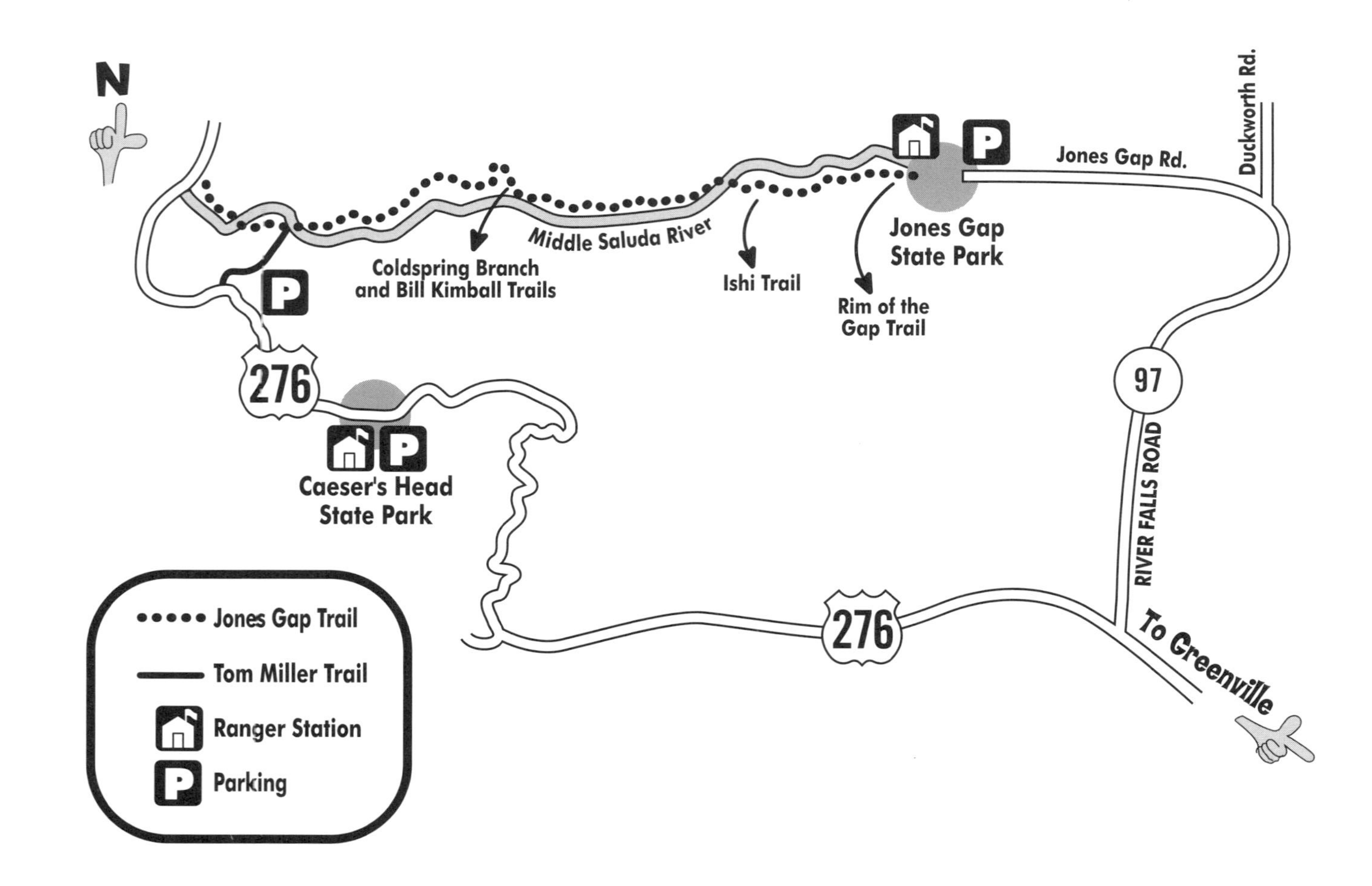
N
Jones Gap Rd.
Duckworth Rd.
Jones Gap State Park
Middle Saluda River
Coldspring Branch and Bill Kimball Trails
Ishi Trail
Rim of the Gap Trail
276
Caeser's Head State Park
97
RIVER FALLS ROAD
276
To Greenville
Jones Gap Trail
Tom Miller Trail
Ranger Station
Parking

Jones Gap Trail

Location: Jones Gap State Park (Greenville County)
Directions: From Greenville, drive north on US 276 to the junction with SC 11 in Cleveland. Continue on US 276 for 1.4 miles and turn right onto River Falls Road (Greenville County S-97) just before the F-Mart convenience store. Drive four miles to the main gate of Jones Gap State Park, and turn right into the designated parking area.
Hiking Time: Approximately 30 minutes
Distance: 5.3 miles (one-way). Many families walk out a short distance to see Jones Gap Falls and backtrack.
Difficulty level: Easy to moderate. The trail is mostly level and flat and crosses several streams (some bridges) as it makes a gradual ascent of more than 1,600 feet. There are no serious obstacles but there are many other longer and more difficult trails here.
Trail surface: Natural. An asphalt path leads past the picnic area and environmental center but the trail crosses a service bridge and quickly becomes a flat, natural surface path.
Trail markings: Blue blazes.
Uses: Hiking, fishing and nature study. The Middle Saluda River runs beside the trail for its entire distance and there are many places along the way to dip your feet in the water.
Facilities: Jones Gap State Park has heated restrooms, drink machines and an environmental learning center. Campsites are available and there are showers.
Best time to visit: Late summer through fall.
Dogs: Yes, on a leash.
Fees: $2 for adults, $1.50 for seniors. It is free for those 15 and younger
Hours: Open daily from 9 a.m. to 6 p.m. (9 p.m. in Daylight Savings Time).
For more information:
Jones Gap State Park
303 Jones Gap Road
Marietta, SC 29661
(864) 836-3647
www.discoversouthcarolina.com

Family Perk

There are few places better for picnics than the tables beside the Middle Saluda River. Children will enjoy the old Cleveland Fish Hatchery which has been restored and stocked with trout.

Photo by Tom Savage.

With access to a handful of waterfalls, a large trail network, the Middle Saluda River and scenic views rivaling any in the East, Jones Gap State Park is among the finest natural wonders of the Upstate. It is one of two state parks that comprise the 10,000-acre Mountain Bridge Wilderness Area (Caesars Head State Park is the other) and part of a 45-mile corridor along the state line that comprises the Blue Ridge Escarpment. The Jones Gap Trail, which is a 5.3-mile one-way trail, is easy, user-friendly and gorgeous – a high priority for families indeed.

The trail actually follows an old toll road that once allowed travelers to pass from River Falls to Caesars Head and beyond to Cedar Mountain, NC. The trail begins near a sign-in kiosk at the main park office and begins meandering up the Middle Saluda River. As you hike, watch for several intersections with trails such as the difficult Rim of the Gap. At approximately 1 mile, you will cross the Middle Saluda River on the John Reid Clonts Bridge which overlooks some very pretty cascades. There are several other waterfalls in the area

Beyond this point, there are more loop options off the Jones Gap Trail. Some of these other trails – including the Coldspring Branch and Bill Kimball Trail – are considerably more difficult than the Jones Gap Trail. One landmark along the main trail is a 50-foot granite outcrop at the 2 mile point that has served as a rain shelter for many families over the years! A number of trailside campsites and some interpretive signs are located along the trail which eventually dead-ends at a brown gate near a small parking area on US 276.

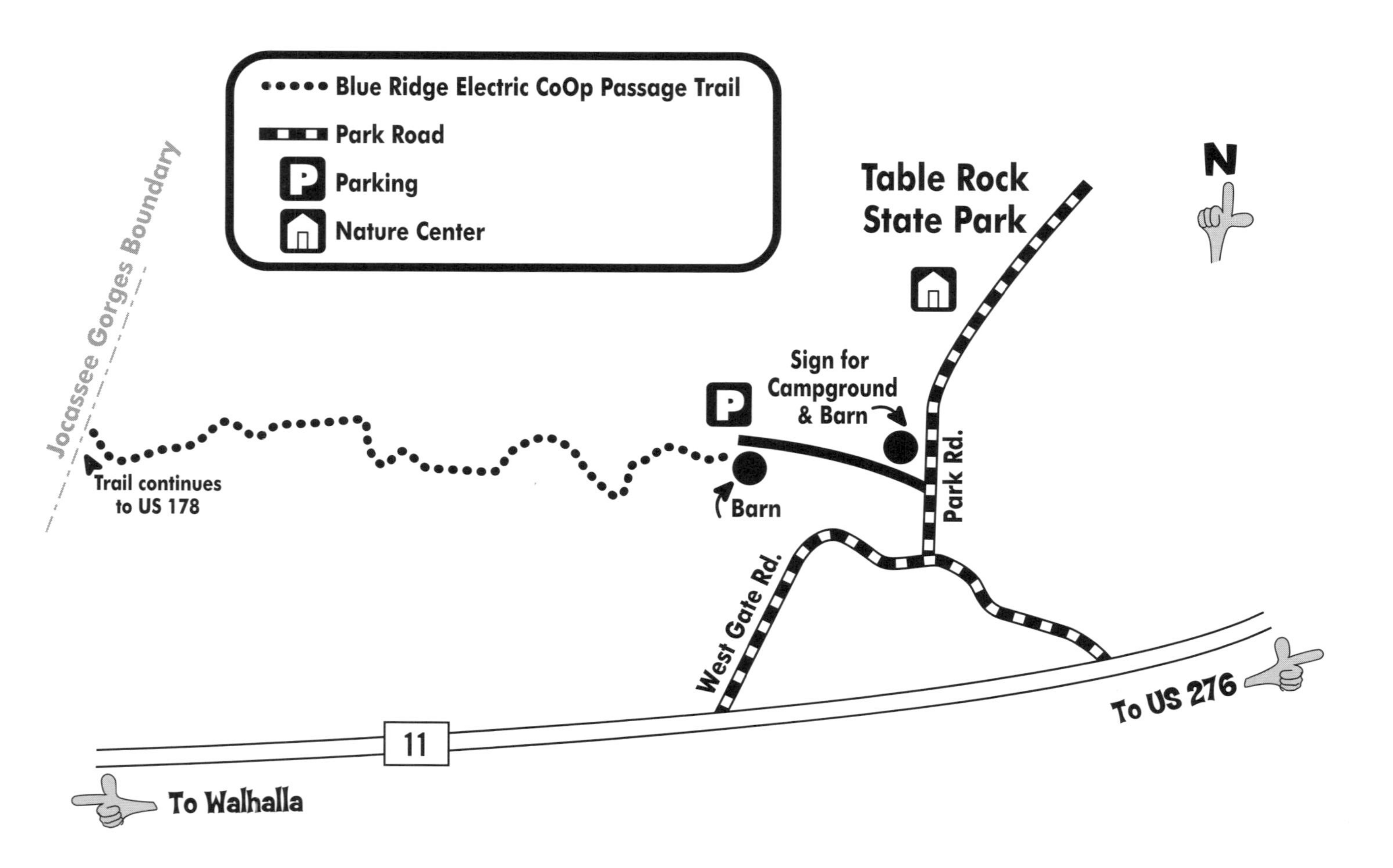

Blue Ridge Electric CoOp Passage Trail
Park Road
Parking
Nature Center
Table Rock
State Park
N
Sign for
Campground
& Barn
Park Rd.
Barn
Jocassee Gorges Boundary
Trail continues
to US 178
West Gate Rd.
11
To US 276
To Walhalla

Blue Ridge Electric CoOp Passage of the Palmetto Trail

7

Location: Table Rock State Park (Pickens County)
Directions: From Greenville, drive north on US 276 to its intersection with SC 11. Veer left (west) onto SC 11 toward Table Rock State Park. Follow to the West Entrance. Turn left at the first signed turn for the campground and The Barn (a meeting facility). The trailhead is located near The Barn.
Hiking Time: About 1.5 hours
Distance: 2 miles
Difficulty level: Moderate
Trail surface: Natural surface, some steep sections and rooty, wet areas. Although the trail follows contours, it is still not easy hiking up this hillside.
Trail markings: Yes, the trail is well signed with yellow blazes.
Uses: Hiking, fishing and seasonal boat rental are available for use on Pinnacle Lake.
Facilities: Restrooms and water are available in the main campground and at the Cherokee Foothills Visitors Center on the south side of SC 11. Drinks and snacks are available from vending machines at the Visitor Center.
Best time to visit: Fall is excellent to see the changing colors of the surrounding forest. The spring wildflower season is also unforgettable.
Dogs: Yes, on a leash.
Fees: $2 for adults; $1.50 for seniors. It is free for those 15 and younger.
Hours: Open daily from 7 a.m. to 9 p.m.
For more information:
Table Rock State Park
158 E Ellison Ln.
Pickens, SC 29671
(864) 878-9813
www.discoversouthcarolina.com

Family Perk

Table Rock naturalists offer curriculum-based science education programs for school children.

Photo by Tom Savage.

The moderately difficult Blue Ridge Electric CoOp Passage of the Palmetto Trail begins from The Barn at Table Rock State Park and travels 2 miles into some rugged mountain terrain. This entire trail actually runs for 12.5 miles but families – especially those with young children – will want to make this an out-and-back trip from Table Rock and ending high on a flank of Pinnacle Mountain at the boundary between the state park and the Jocassee Gorges, a 44,000-acrea property managed by the S.C. Department of Natural Resources.

The trail, which was made possible in part through funding from the Pickens-based electric utility and security system provider, Blue Ridge Electric CoOp, is a meandering trip into a part of Table Rock State Park few have seen. From the trailhead, the path wanders over several ridges and crosses a stream in the adjacent Wesleyan Camp before beginning a long ascent. The trail follows rolling contours and climbs through many coves that are home to an astonishing array of wildflowers and wildlife such as wild turkey, fox and even black bear. In a final series of switchbacks up to a flank of Pinnacle Mountain, the trail gains several hundred feet of elevation to an overlook area with excellent views of the Piedmont in the winter and early spring. Once the trail joins the Jocassee Gorges property, it follows an improved logging road west for several miles toward Camp Adger. The park boundary is well marked and is a good turnaround point for those who do not wish to hike further.

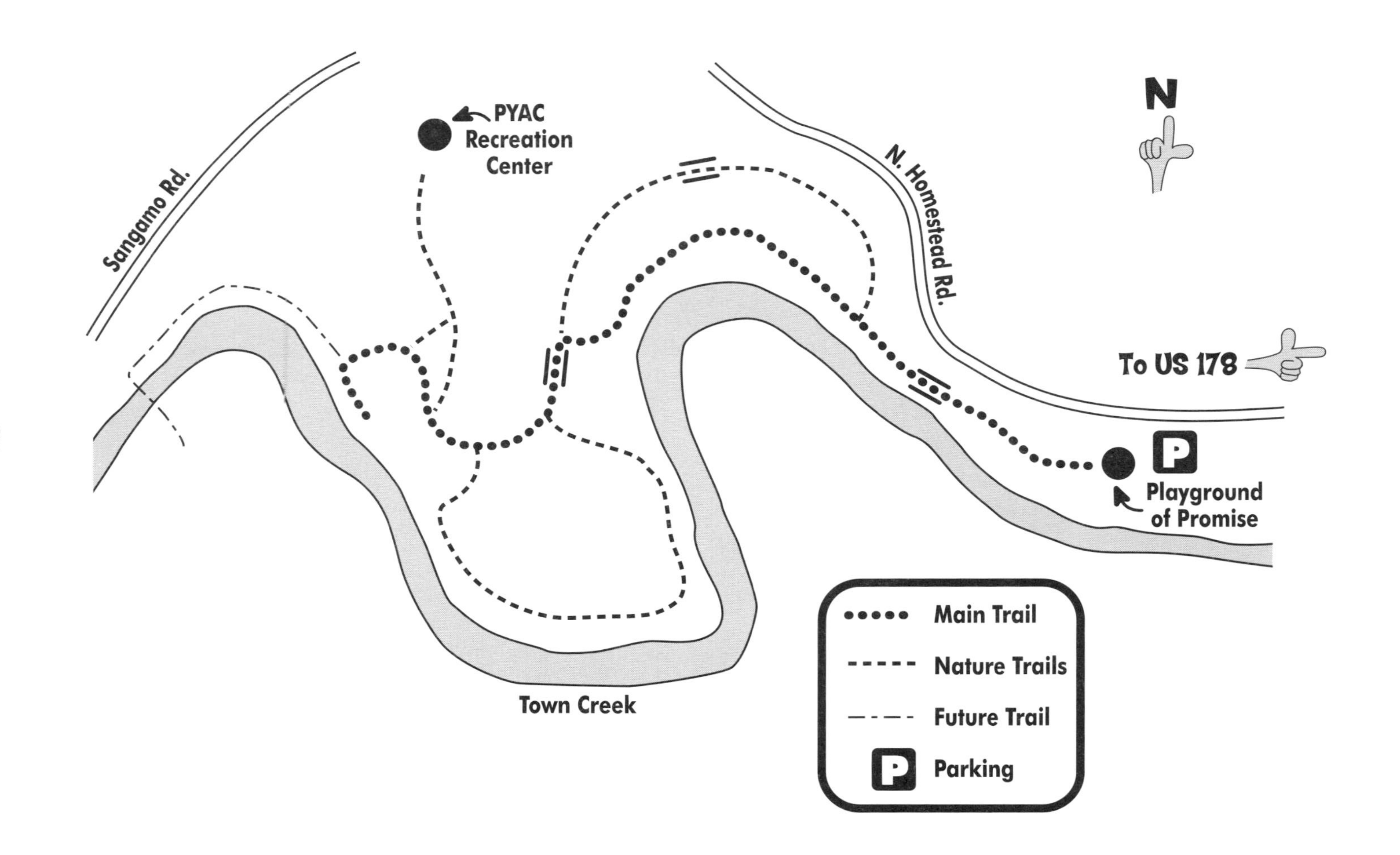
PYAC Recreation Center
Sangamo Rd.
N. Homestead Rd.
N
To US 178
Playground of Promise
Town Creek
Main Trail
Nature Trails
Future Trail
Parking
P

Town Creek Trail

Location: Jaycee Park and the Playground of Promise (Pickens County)
Directions: From Main Street in Pickens take SC 178 north. Signs will direct you to a left turn onto N. Homestead Road. Follow a short distance to parking.
Hiking Time: 30 minutes to 1.5 hours
Distance: Nearly 2 miles of interconnecting multi-use trails.
Difficulty level: Easy to moderate
Trail surface: Natural surface trail with some uneven areas and short hills.
Trail markings: The trail is well marked and signed.
Uses: Hiking and biking
Facilities: Restrooms and water are available near the playground, and baseball facilities.
Best time to visit: A well-timed fall visit to Pickens County will make you consider moving here; the annual Pumpkin Festival in October in nearby Pumpkintown is a treat.
Dogs: Yes, on a leash.
Fees: None
Hours: Dawn to dusk
For more information:
Pickens City Hall
PO Box 217
Pickens, SC 29671
(864) 878-6421

Family Perk

The "Playground of Promise," located at the parking area for Town Creek Park, is among the best parks in the Upstate with structures for all ages and abilities.

With nearly 2 miles of mostly easy to moderate connecting trails, the Town Creek Trail system in Pickens County offers great opportunities for active families. But a key reason to visit Town Creek Park is stopping by the wonderful Playground of Promise, which sprawls around the entrance to the trails and offers unique play structures for children of all ages.

The Town Creek Trails, adjacent to the scenic Town Creek, were built on a gently rolling, wooded 43-acre site donated by Shlumberger Industries. Trails loop through the woods and end up back at the parking area; getting lost shouldn't be a concern. Local walkers, runners and students from nearby Pickens High School are often out strolling on the trail and many of these same people also contribute to its maintenance. The surrounding woods are home to deer and the occasional black bear that makes its way down from the mountains in northern Pickens County.

Probably the single most noteworthy feature of the Town Creek Trail is the fact that much of the corridor follows the rail bed of the Appalachian Lumber Company's narrow gauge railroad, which

was in operation around 1928. The railroad ran from the sawmill, currently in operation behind Ingles, north to the far reaches of the Eastatoee Valley and nearly to Rocky Bottom. Hikers can still see the "corduroy effect" in some stretches of the trail. This rippled effect in the footpath is a vestige of the practice of laying logs and poles, usually black locust, in boggy places along rail bed. Hikers will also notice a series of bridges that span the former gaps and swales that the train track traversed as it worked its way around the slopes and steep grades.

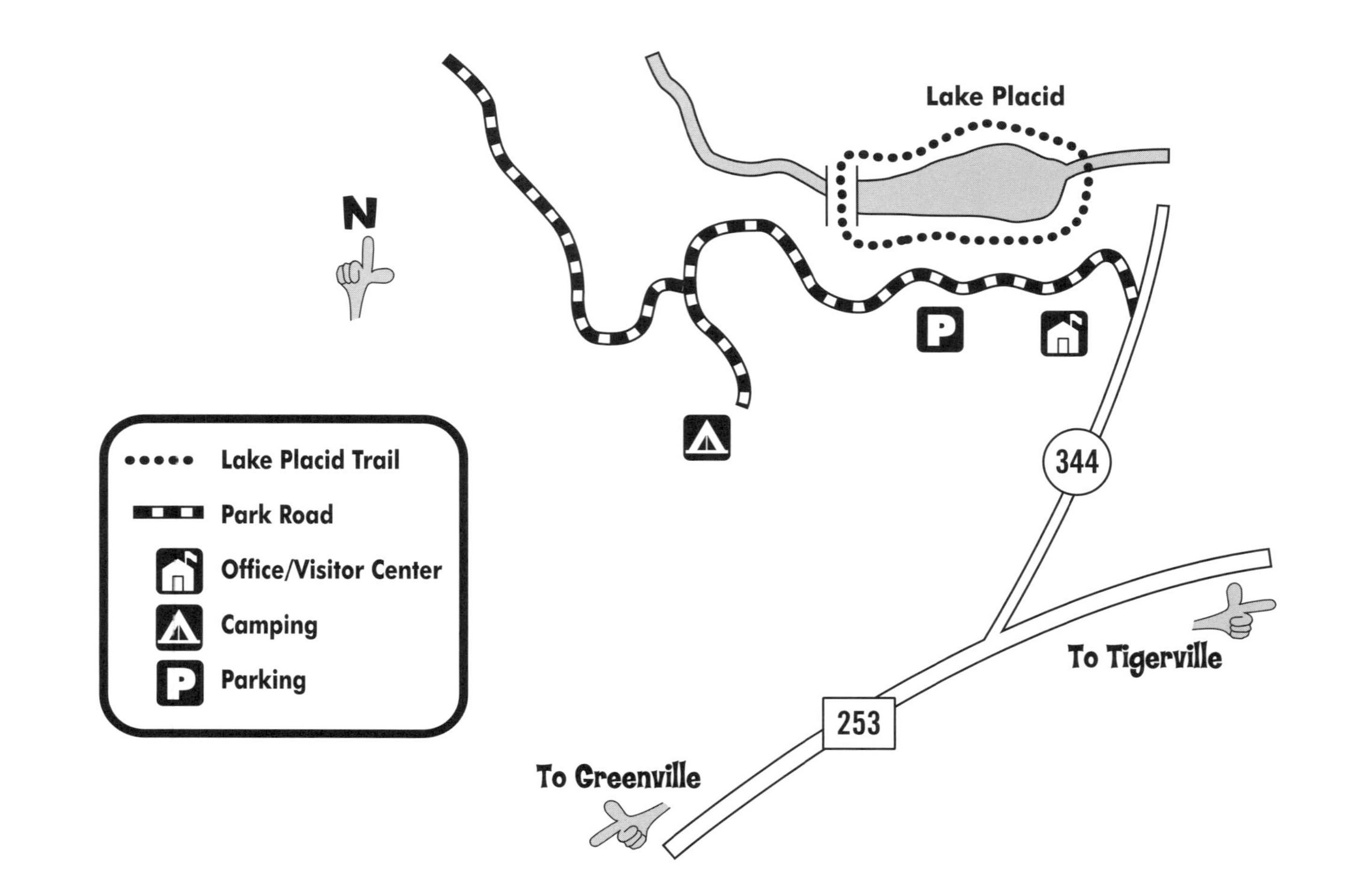
Lake Placid
N
344
253
To Tigerville
To Greenville
Lake Placid Trail
Park Road
Office/Visitor Center
Camping
Parking

Lake Placid Trail

Location: Paris Mountain State Park (Greenville County)
Directions: From Greenville, drive north on US 276. At the intersection of SC 253, turn right and bear left at the next light to stay on SC 253. Drive 2.5 miles and turn left onto State Park Road (S-23-344). The park entrance is on the left. From the entrance, drive a short distance to the picnic shelter and parking area on the right.
Hiking Time: Approximately 30 minutes
Distance: 1.2-mile loop trail around the lake
Difficulty level: Easy
Trail surface: Natural, mostly flat and level.
Trail markings: While the trail is not formally marked, the tread is well defined and impossible to lose sight of.
Uses: Hiking, birding, swimming, boating
Facilities: Several picnic areas and restroom facilities. A bathhouse is available near the lake.
Best time to visit: Summer offers the best opportunity to enjoy this trail. After a stroll around the lake take a dip in the park's swimming area.
Dogs: Yes, on a leash.
Fees: $2 per adults, $1.25 for seniors and free for those 15 and younger.
Hours: 9 a.m. to 6 p.m. (extended to 8 p.m. on Fridays). Hours are extended daily to 9 p.m. during Daylight Savings Time. Park office hours are 11 a.m. to noon and 4 to 5 p.m.
For more information:
Paris Mountain State Park
2401 State Park Road
Greenville, SC 29609
(864) 244-5565
www.parismountain.com/sp

Family Perk

Paris Mountain has an excellent slate of interpretive programs. Call ahead for details but a favorite is the Aquatic Habitat Hike, which includes collecting animal species in Mountain Creek and examining them later by microscope.

Photo by Ned Cannon.

Located conveniently on the outskirts of Greenville, local residents have enjoyed Paris Mountain State Park as a popular retreat area since it opened in 1937. The park's many recreation trails, camping and swimming facilities provide upstate residents with unique outdoor recreation options today, especially as the park staff works diligently to build new trails and rehabilitate many old favorites. Paris Mountain has some excellent, multi-use loop trails but if your family is new to the outdoors, the Lake Placid Nature Trail may be your best option. The easy, 1.2-mile trail loops around the park lake, offers many access points and affords families an easy, accessible place to hike.

One nice bonus of the Lake Placid Trail is that it also offers access to many side trails leading to the shoreline and even a man-made waterfall created by an old dam at the far end of the lake. One spur trail takes you to the ruins of an amphitheater while others meander off into the woods. Along the way, be sure to keep an eye out for wildlife that inhabit the area, while also using the interpretive signs to identify a wide variety of plant life. If you stop at the park office or fee booth, make sure to ask for either the Lake Placid Self-Guided Nature Trail Brochure or the Self-Guided Math Trail Brochure, which has directions to eight marked stations along the trail where children and adults can do math-related activities.

Once you have finished your hike, if the weather is warm enough, make sure to visit the old Lake Placid boathouse and swim in the roped-off area. Visitors can rent kayaks, canoes, and paddle boats ($3 per half hour). The many picnic tables around the lake make it a good place for a family outing.

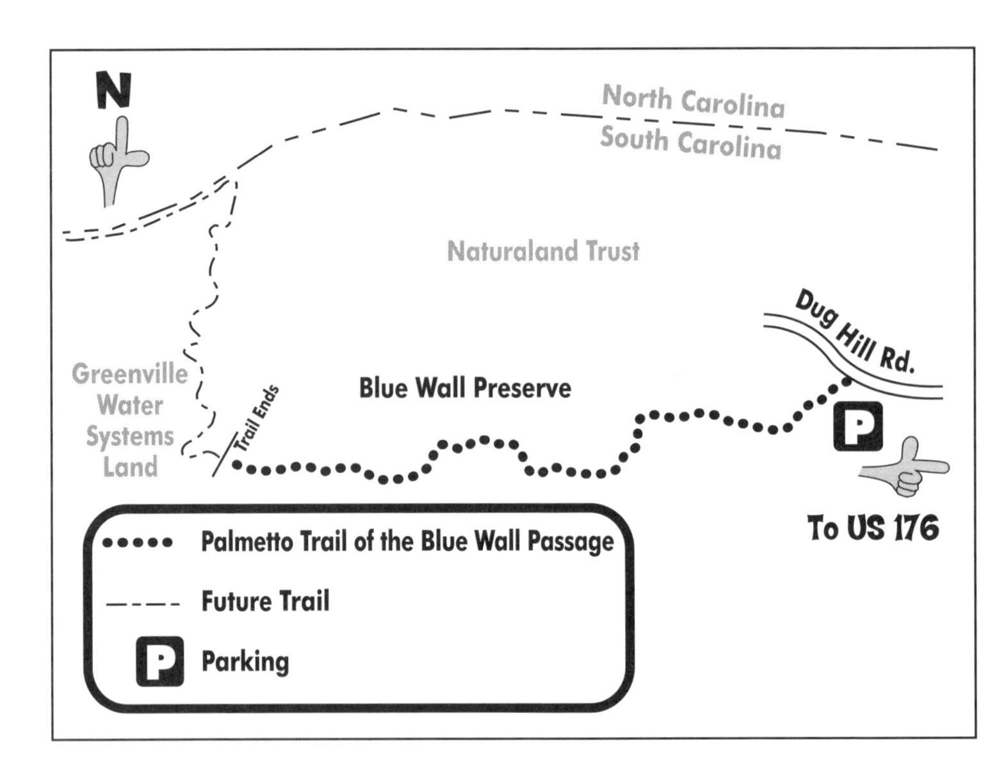
N
North Carolina
South Carolina
Naturaland Trust
Dug Hill Rd.
Greenville Water Systems Land
Trail Ends
Blue Wall Preserve
To US 176
Palmetto Trail of the Blue Wall Passage
Future Trail
Parking

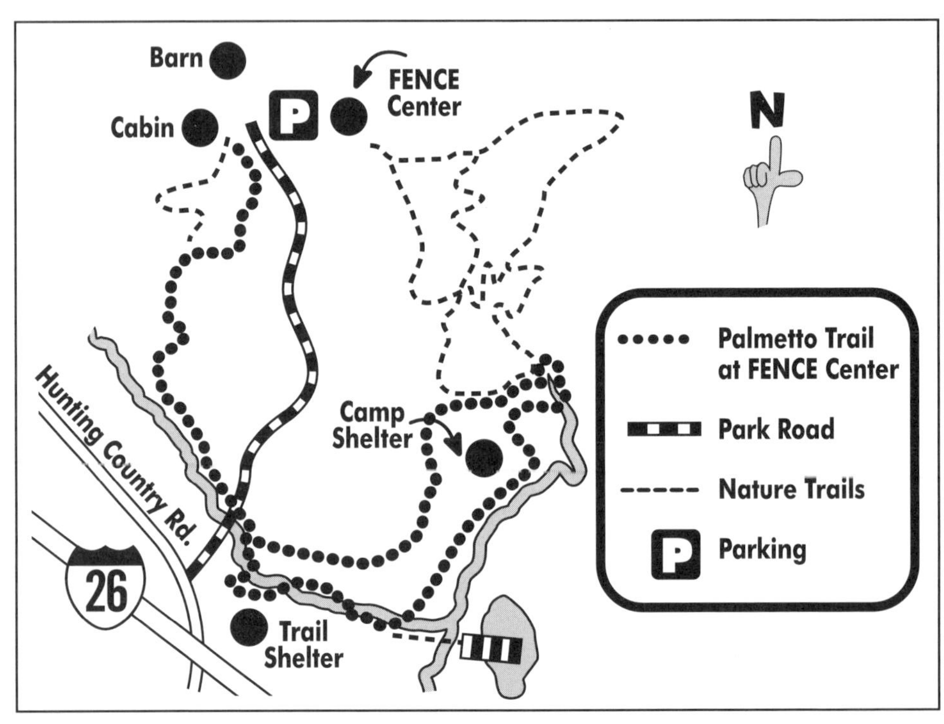
Barn
FENCE Center
Cabin
N
Hunting Country Rd.
Camp Shelter
26
Trail Shelter
Palmetto Trail at FENCE Center
Park Road
Nature Trails
Parking

Blue Wall Passage of the Palmetto Trail

Location: Two separate trailheads

1. Nature Conservancy's Blue Wall Preserve (Greenville County)

Directions: From Landrum to the Blue Wall Preserve, drive north on US 176 toward Tryon, NC. Drive 2 miles and turn left onto Lakeshore Drive. Cross a bridge and follow West Lakeshore Drive around the lake to Dug Hill Road. Turn left and look for a small, signed parking area on the left. From the parking area, follow the road across an old bridge to the trailhead.

2. Foothills Equestrian Center (FENCE) (Polk County, NC)

Directions: From Landrum to FENCE, drive east on SC 14 to signs for FENCE at a left onto Bomar Road. Follow one short block to Prince Road and turn right. Drive 1.7 miles on Prince Road to a Hunting Country Road on the left (just before a bridge over Interstate 26). Follow 0.6 miles to the entrance for FENCE on the right; signs lead you to the Palmetto Trail trailhead.

Hiking Time: 3 hours (complete) for Blue Wall Preserve, can be reduced.
1 hour for FENCE, can be extended.

Distance: 6 miles total (round trip) at Blue Wall Preserve, can be reduced.
3 miles at FENCE, additional loops including a newer 1-mile trail called the Connelly Connector.

Difficulty level: Moderate at Blue Wall Preserve if you don't make the climb to Vaughns Gap. Hard otherwise. Easy to moderate at FENCE.

Trail surface: Rugged logging roads and rocky trails at Blue Wall Preserve. Many uneven sections and steep, narrow switchbacks near the Gap. Natural surface at FENCE, with well-maintained trails and boardwalks over ponds.

Family Perk

In summertime, FENCE offers educational camps on astronomy, nature study and outdoor schools. The camps are inexpensive and great for active children.

Trail markings: Yes, at Blue Wall Preserve and FENCE, yellow upside down exclamation marks and Palmetto Trail markings.

Uses: Hiking, birding.

Facilities: No facilities at the Blue Wall Preserve.
Restrooms available at FENCE nature center.

Best time to visit: Fall

Dogs: Yes, on a leash.

Fees: None. Donations suggested at FENCE

Hours: Dawn to dusk at Blue Wall Preserve
FENCE is open daily from 9 a.m. to 5 p.m.

Photo by Oliver Buckles.

For more information:

The Nature Conservancy	FENCE
P.O. Box 232	3381 Hunting Country Rd.
Greenville, SC 29602	Tryon, NC 28782
(864) 233-4988	(828) 859-9021
www.nature.org	www.fence.org

The Blue Wall Passage of the Palmetto Trail is actually an on-road corridor connecting two separate and very different off-road hiking destinations. At one end, the Nature Conservancy's Blue Wall Preserve offers a remote, wilderness-walking opportunity with stunning views of the 3,188-foot Hogback Mountain. At the other is the Foothills Equestrian Nature Center (FENCE), an equestrian and environmental education center just over the state line in North Carolina with well-maintained, easy walking paths and access to facilities.

The 3-mile, one-way hike at the Blue Wall Preserve begins with a gradual ascent along an old roadbed from the trailhead and passing Twin Ponds. This area features spectacular views of the steep mountain slopes towering above the trail and affords some excellent opportunities for bird watching. The trail begins in cove hardwoods and moves into a mixed hardwood forest with hemlock and rhododendron thickets as you climb up towards Vaughns Gap. Soon after passing Twin Ponds (at about the 1.25-mile point) there is a primitive campground on the right where families may want to spread out and enjoy an evening under the stars.

After this campsite, the trail soon passes a City of Landrum water intake, which is a nice spot to lounge under tall trees and along the gurgling waters of Vaughn's Creek. The trail climbs over a rocky section and begins ascending much more steeply at this point; in winter and spring, the views from Vaughns Gap are excellent. The trail dead-ends into the Greenville Watershed, which is strictly monitored private property, so please backtrack at the turnaround point.

FENCE has more than 5 miles of trails including sheltered walking paths, an asphalt trail for those with mobility impairments and a nature pond with an observation boardwalk for bird watching and wildlife viewing. The trailhead for some of the best trails is just inside the main entrance and begins from an old cabin and shelter and continues down to the nature pond. Maps are available at the Nature Center.

Midlands & Piedmont

Text by Amanda Capps

For the purposes of this book, the Midlands and Piedmont section includes hikes from southern Spartanburg County down nearly to the Coastal Plain – portions of 30 counties. Visitors all too often write off this area when visiting South Carolina, preferring to consider it a sandy swath with little to offer active, adventuresome families. Nothing could be farther from the truth. In fact, the Midlands and Piedmont offers a wide variety of family hiking opportunities.

For instance, although it has neither a beach nor a scenic mountain range, Aiken County is the Midlands' answer to a resort community. Refined recreation in the form of horse racing, polo and fox hunting became permanent facets of Aiken's culture in the late 1800s as wealthy Northerners migrated south. Today, wide streets, massive trees and azaleas add to the aesthetic appeal that many towns of all sizes strive to emulate. Aiken is a reflection of the "Old, Deep South" and all of its idealized connotations. It is a relaxed culture, but one that takes its recreation seriously. Aiken has 24 parks, two heritage preserves and a serene wildlife sanctuary within easy driving distance. On South Carolina's western border, the "Freshwater Coast" along the Savannah River offers miles of recreation. In order to solve flooding problems with the Savannah in the 1940s, the U.S. Army Corps of Engineers built a dam, creating the 70,000-acre Lake Thurmond. Formerly known as Clarks Hill Lake, McCormick County's Lake Thurmond is the second-largest manmade lake in Southeast. Featuring 1,200 miles of shoreline, Lake Thurmond's two main attractions are Hickory Knob State Resort Area and Baker Creek State Park.

Closer to the geographic center of the state, one visit to Congaree National Park will inspire an infatuation with nature. One of the more preferable vistas is the Congaree Bluffs Heritage Preserve, a 201-acre tract directly across the Congaree River from the Monument. This Calhoun County site on the river's south side offers added protection for the Monument, along with breathtaking views of up to 20 miles on clear days. Urban and suburban trails in the Columbia area such as the Three Rivers Greenway and Saluda Shoals Park provide excellent opportunities for diversion while your family attends a football game, convention or work-related function.

Note! *While there are many family friendly opportunities available throughout the Midlands and Piedmont, it is important to remember that we focused on just a few areas close to the trails in this book. Make sure that you do plenty of exploring too!*

Detours *No family-oriented hiking trip is complete without stopping off either en route or on the way home for ice cream, folksy stories, good food or educational opportunities. Here are just a few family-oriented locations in the Midlands and near our favorite family walking trails.*

Laurens County

(For hikes #11-12: Glenn Springs Passage of the Palmetto Trail, Horseshoe Falls. See also the Mountains section.)

In Laurens County, the town of Clinton is home to Presbyterian College, an attractive and well-respected liberal arts school. Overnight visitors will definitely want to see The Farmhouse at Bush River, just outside the city. "Casual elegance" is a term that begins to describe the house and grounds, but it falls short of defining this amiable estate. One guest said a stay at Bush River is like a luxurious trip to the Irish countryside, but it is as comfortable as your favorite relative's home. Guest rooms are not ideally suited for children, but families passing through the area will want to call ahead and make arrangements to see the farm's star attractions – dozens of beautiful alpaca. Their comical faces and domesticated demeanor invite affection, while their lush fur lends itself to some of the softest sweaters and scarves on the planet. These items are for sale in a small shop adjacent to the farm.

Approximately 10 miles north on US 76, the county seat of Laurens has a majestic Courthouse Square. The building itself – with its massive Greek Revival columns – sits atop wide sets of stairs on each side. In its own rite, the building is as august and well-preserved as the State House or any such historic building in the area. Approaching the square from US 76, visitors will see Little River Brewing Company where patrons can dine on the patio overlooking Little River. There is also a short walking trail that is lighted in the evenings. On the far side of Courthouse Square, West Main Street is the address for some of the most stately Southern homes and churches in the area.

Built in 1846, the Church of the Epiphany is the oldest Episcopal Church in the state. Its doors are open for private prayer 24 hours a day. A must-see for children and adults is the Artist's Coop, also located on the public square. Self-guided tours of the shop and galleries are free of charge. The coop features media from watercolor to handcrafted jewelry, and inspirations range from South Carolina to the rest of the globe. On a good day, an artist staff member may talk with children and spare a few minutes for an impromptu lesson. Visitors could find an irresistible souvenir or a new passion at the coop.

York, Chester and Lancaster Counties

(For hikes #13-14: Lake Haigler Trail and Canal Trail)

In Lancaster County, travelers who enjoy the elegance of a bed and breakfast will want to see Kilburnie - The Inn at Craig Farm. It is the oldest residence in Lancaster and has five rooms - all bearing the name of someone who has had an impact on our nation's history. Generously sized rooms with king-sized beds, whirlpool baths and fireplaces are available. The President Andrew Jackson Suite even has a fireplace in the bathroom, but the rates are reasonable enough for a lesser official to afford. Also on the grounds are formal gardens and a half-mile nature walk. Waxhaw Presbyterian Church Cemetery, a popular spot for genealogical research, is nearby.

The public square in downtown Chester is known as The Hill, but the view of this unique layout is worth the steep climb. Chester is a wealth of century-old architecture, but downtown revitalization efforts led to the development of upstairs apartments and many new shops. At the top of Monument Square, there is a cistern that was discovered during construction in 1996. These vessels were used to collect rainwater until 1897 when a public water system was built. There is also a Civil War era cannon unearthed in 1986. Only 24 of its kind are still known to be in existence.

Historic Brattonsville, near Rock Hill in York County, is a world unto itself. The York County Historical Society developed this makeshift village of 18th and 19th century structures as its Bicentennial project. Some of the buildings were moved from other locations and thoughtfully restored for public viewing. The grounds cover more than 700 acres and include 29 historic structures, along with the Walt Schrader Trails, eight miles of hiking, bicycling and horseback riding paths. Brattonsville hosts several festivals throughout the year, including Red Hills Farm Day, the Battle of Huck's Defeat, and the annual Christmas Tour.

Richland, Lexington, Saluda and Sumter Counties

(For hikes #15, #16, #17, #18 and #19: Saluda Shoals Park, Three Rivers Greenway, Boardwalk Loop, Coquina Nature Trail, Swan Lake-Iris Gardens)

Family walking trips in the Midlands all center around the state capital, Columbia, so that seems a logical place to start our driving detours. Even native South Carolinians will appreciate a side trip through downtown Columbia.

Columbia is resplendent with "sandlapper" history, but it has its eclectic side as well. The recently revitalized Congaree Vista, an area that lies along Gervais between Huger and Assembly streets, is evidence that Columbia is a vibrant city that has evolved with a cosmopolitan flair. Antiques, art and nightlife characterize this stylish section of town. Fall, particularly November, is an ideal time for this trip, as surrounding destinations including Congaree National Park, Three Rivers Greenway and Saluda Shoals Park all reach prime season for walking, and candles light up the Vista. Merchants keep later hours and artists perform and show during Vista Lights, an annual nod to the rebirth of that area.

Also of note is Riverbanks Zoo. Conveniently situated at Greystone Boulevard off Interstate 126, it is another means of accessing nature at its finest. A 70-acre botanical garden and an awe-inspiring 60,000-gallon aquarium are two of the main attractions. Yet every inch of Riverbanks is a peaceful pleasure, as the animals thrive in realistic environments. Visitors are transported to other worlds as they enter and exit various habitats, while large residents of Riverbanks enjoy life without bars and cages. A few hundred yards are the difference between an exotic journey to the Amazon and a rustic trip to the dairy farmer's barn.

In Saluda County, the Monetta Drive-in, better known as "The Big Mo," is the last of its kind in South Carolina – and one of only a handful in the country. Unlike some attractions revived in the name of "retro" fads, the drive-in is a thriving business that just happens to give the contented feeling of bygone years. Sausage dogs are popular items at the concessions stand, and patrons look forward to movie trivia during 20-minute intermissions. The Big Mo carries current features and is usually open only on Fridays and Saturdays during warm weather months. Guests are advised to arrive 30 minutes before show time (around 8:20 p.m.). The Big Mo is definitely a place for family fun. Kids can walk and play on the lawn, which is typically scattered with chairs and blankets. Admission is extremely reasonable – $5 for age 12 and older, $1 for ages 4-11, and free for children under four years old. The drive-in is located 20 miles east of Aiken on US 1 at the Aiken and Saluda County line (seven miles from I-20 at Exit 33).

McCormick, Abbeville, Greenwood & Aiken Counties

(For hike #20: Cathedral Aisle Trail)

Like so many small towns in the Palmetto State, McCormick runs parallel to the railroad tracks that gave it life in the 19th century. However, unlike other towns, it is built over miles of gold mines that drew the first settlers. Each year in September, McCormick commemorates its history with the Gold Rush Days Festival. Concerts, carnival rides and classic car shows are typical events, but where else can visitors go panning for gold? Also on Main Street in McCormick is "The Mack" or McCormick Arts Council at the Keturah. Many years have passed since visitors found lodging at the old Keturah Hotel, but today, they find artwork from both local artists and outside exhibitors. The Gallery Shop sells local work and souvenirs. Also, watch for news of concerts and plays in the nearby city park and amphitheater.

After a stroll through old-world streets of downtown, tourists will find there is much more to McCormick County for nature lovers beyond walking trails. By following the Savannah River Scenic Highway (SC 81 and US 221/SC 28), which runs the entire length of the county, there are numerous stores for ice, bait etc. Also on that route, Rubbie's is the place to go for barbecue and – as the locals say, "If the smoker's on, you know he's open."

Abbeville is known as both the cradle and the deathbed of the Confederacy. The first secessionist meeting was held there, and on May 2, 1865, Confederate President Jefferson Davis held his last council of war meeting at the home of Maj. Armistead Burt, the Burt-Stark House, which is located at 400 N. Main Street and within walking distance of downtown. Heading away from the beautiful brick streets of Town Square, visitors will soon spot the Greek Revival mansion sitting behind a grove of lush magnolia trees. The house splits a wide street, acting as a focal point and a gateway for the many architecturally significant homes in the area. It is open from 1 to 5 p.m. on Fridays and Saturdays throughout the year, and there is a small admission fee.

There are several other appealing options downtown, but one of the most popular restaurants in the area is Yoder's, a diner-type establishment with Pennsylvania Dutch fare. For a more casual meal with the whole family, it is down-home cooking with a twist. Located on SC 72 between Greenwood and Abbeville, Yoder's is open Wednesday through Saturday with a lunch buffet and smorgasbord style dinners. The cooks can do almost anything with a casserole, as the menu piques curiosity with offerings like pineapple or eggplant dishes. But, desserts like "shoo-fly" pie, fresh strawberry pie, date nut pudding, egg custard and apple fritter sundaes make any side trip worthwhile.

Emerald Farm, located in eastern Greenwood County, is a working farm of 20 much-loved Saanen goats. Owner Kathryn Zahn likes to tell visitors that it is really a "funny farm" because fun is the order of the day on the 50-acre site that also features an intricate kingdom of model railroad tracks, a BMX track and a landing strip for remote-controlled model airplanes. Children and adults enjoy meeting the affectionate herd of Swiss farm animals that produce the milk for homemade cheese, ice cream and soap. The "soap shack" produces and sells additional items including souvenir bars shaped like goats. The Emerald Farm Railroad Clubhouse is available for viewing, but for those who want to ride a train, "all aboard" is the signal to hop on the Union Pacific replica that tours the grounds. The good news for families is that a visit to the farm is truly a free ride. With the exception of gift and hobby shop purchases, there is no charge for fun.

"Thoroughbred Country" is another name for Aiken County, where the sandy soil is ideal for training horses. Visitors can see magnificent animals and their trainers at work. Early mornings are the best hours to stop by Aiken Training Track on Powderhouse Road off South Boundary Avenue, Aiken Mile Track on Banks Mill Road or Whitney Polo Field on Mead Avenue. The Equestrian District is easy to identify by the dirt roads, which protect horses' hooves. The Aiken Triple Crown is staged over three successive Saturdays in March. The Trials are held at Aiken Training Track.

The former home of Mr. And Mrs. C. Oliver Iselin no longer exists, but Hopeland Garden is a perpetual gift from the family to the city and all who visit. Hopeland holds Story Time for children up to age 12 each Tuesday at 4 p.m. during the months of March, April and May. Hopeland Gardens is open year-round from 10 a.m. to sunset. The Hall of Fame is open from 2 p.m. to 5 p.m. Tuesday to Sunday from September through May, and The Dollhouse is open from 2 p.m. to 5 p.m. on Sundays.

For more information

Artist's Coop (803) 984-9359
Aiken Chamber of Commerce (803) 641-1111
Belmont Inn (877) 459-8118
Chester Downtown Development Association (803) 581-2222
Columbia Metropolitan Convention and Visitors Bureau (803) 254-0479
Congaree Vista (803) 256-1873
Dupont Planetarium (803) 641-3558
Emerald Farm (888) 290-9246
Greater Abbeville Chamber of Commerce (864) 366-4600
Greenwood County Chamber of Commerce (864) 223-8431
Historic Brattonsville (803) 684-2327
Historical Aiken Tours and Turnabout Farms (803) 593-8000
Hopeland Gardens (803) 642-7630
Kilburnie –The Inn at Craig Farm (803) 416-8420
Little Red Barn Pottery Art & Antiques (803) 541-7900
MACK Art Gallery (864) 465-3216
McCormick County Chamber of Commerce (864) 465-2835
Riverbanks Zoo and Botanical Gardens (803) 779-8717
Monetta Drive-in (803) 685-7949
The Farylwuse at Busy River (804) 833-3881
Thurmond Lake Visitors Center (864) 333-1100
York County Convention and Visitors Bureau (800) 866-5200

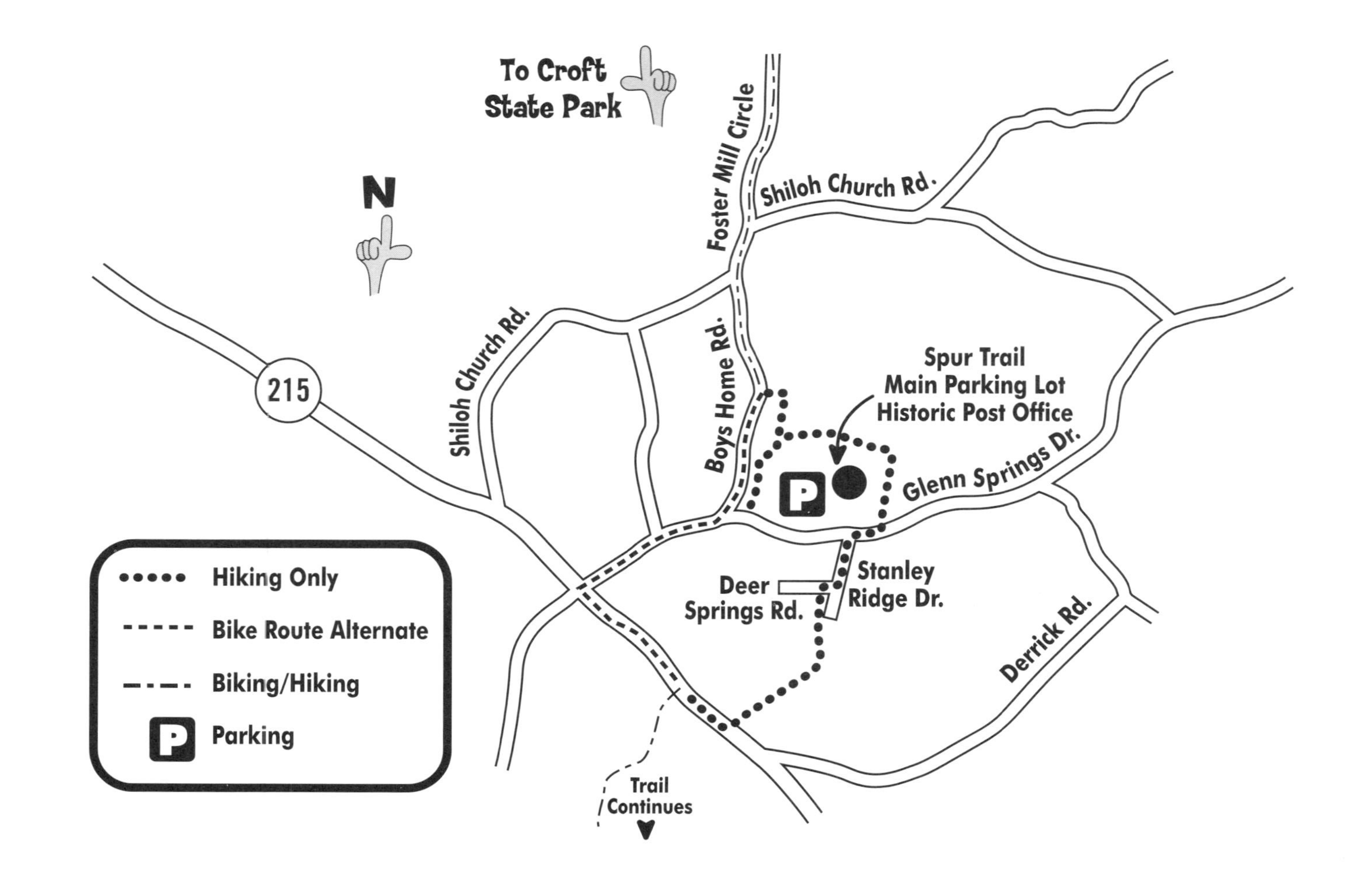
To Croft
State Park
N
Foster Mill Circle
Shiloh Church Rd.
215
Shiloh Church Rd.
Boys Home Rd.
Spur Trail
Main Parking Lot
Historic Post Office
Glenn Springs Dr.
Deer
Springs Rd.
Stanley
Ridge Dr.
Derrick Rd.
Trail
Continues
Hiking Only
Bike Route Alternate
Biking/Hiking
Parking

Glenn Springs Passage of the Palmetto Trail

Location: Glenn Springs (Spartanburg County)
Directions: From Spartanburg, drive south on SC 56 to the community of Pauline and turn left onto SC 215. Drive approximately 2 miles to Glenn Springs and turn left onto SC 150 (Glenn Springs Road). Continue 0.5 miles to the post office and park.
Hiking Time: About 1 hour
Distance: 2 miles (one way). The entire trail is 7 miles one way with a parking drop-off available at the southern terminus on Stagecoach Road.
Difficulty level: Easy if you do the short section; moderate otherwise.
Trail surface: Natural surface with some rock and wooden steps, a bridge and one ankle-high creek ford required. The northern section of the trail connects to Croft State Natural Area via a dirt road.
Trail markings: White blazes signify a "spur" of the Palmetto Trail from the main trailhead to the intersection with the main trail. Once on the main trail, look for yellow blazes.
Uses: Hiking, mountain biking (limited use). Please note that this trail is located on private property. Users are required to stay on the designated trail at all times.
Facilities: None
Best time to visit: Early spring is a great time to view wildflowers and scenic sections of this Piedmont forest. Fall is spectacular.
Dogs: Yes, on a leash
Fees: None
Hours: Dawn to dusk
For more information:
Palmetto Conservation Foundation
P.O. Box 1984
Spartanburg, SC 29304
(864) 948-9615
www.palmettoconservation.org

Family Perk

Four local churches in the Spatanburg area have adopted this trail and use it regularly for walking programs. More information available at the trailhead.

Photo by Diane Lambert.

An easy, 2-mile out-and-back stretch of the Glenn Springs Passage is one of the most historic sections of the statewide Palmetto Trail. The picturesque town of Glenn Springs became one of South Carolina's most popular vacation spots in the latter half of the 19th century as legends spread about its natural mineral springs and the supposed healing powers they contained. In those days, trips to the beautiful, wooded environs of Glenn Springs were simple: Folks would journey by train from Spartanburg to a luxury, four-story hotel that dominated the landscape in those days. People would take the mineral spring water in the morning and then walk along wooded natural paths or relax on rocking chairs on the hotel veranda until parties would strike up each evening. The hotel burned to the ground in 1941. But today, 20 buildings listed on the National Register of Historic Places serve as reminders of this community's bygone glory days. The ruins of the hotel - rubble and glass bottles of spring water - are still visible off Glenn Springs Road.

Today, many families journey here just to see the stately old mansions and walk along the Glenn Springs Passage, which begins from a parking lot across from Calvary Episcopal Church (and near the historic post office). Follow the trail through a stately Piedmont forest past several benches and a rain shelter to a large bridge over a gurgling creek. The spur forms a "T" intersection at which you can walk north (left) or south (right).

The southern route treks through a shady, mixed hardwood forest with scenic views of farmers' meadows, narrow gorges and many creek crossings. This trail was made possible by many local landowners who opened their property to visitors; please respect their wishes by staying on the trail path. The northern route follows paths that may have once been used by vacationers at the hotel and eventually joins Foster Mill Road at a berm where a two-car railroad train once carried passengers on a nine-mile trip from Roebuck to the hotel.

Although the trail may feel remote today, four local church congregations who regularly visit the area for walking activities and events have adopted it. Watch for folks on the trail or you can find information about their walking programs at the trailhead.

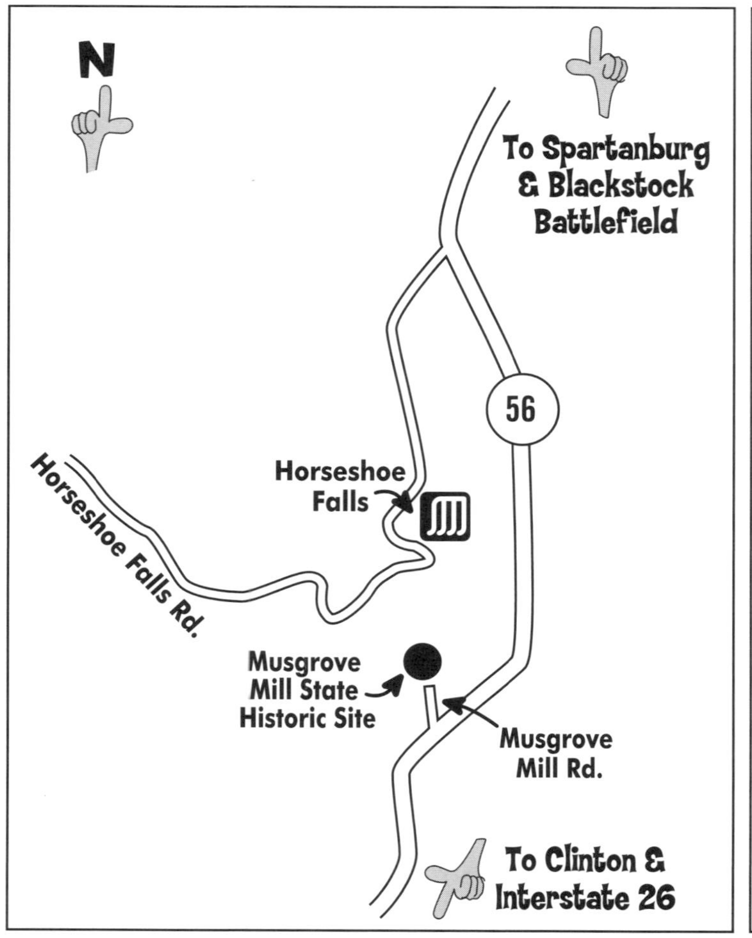
N
To Spartanburg
& Blackstock
Battlefield
56
Horseshoe
Falls
Horseshoe Falls Rd.
Musgrove
Mill State
Historic Site
Musgrove
Mill Rd.
To Clinton &
Interstate 26

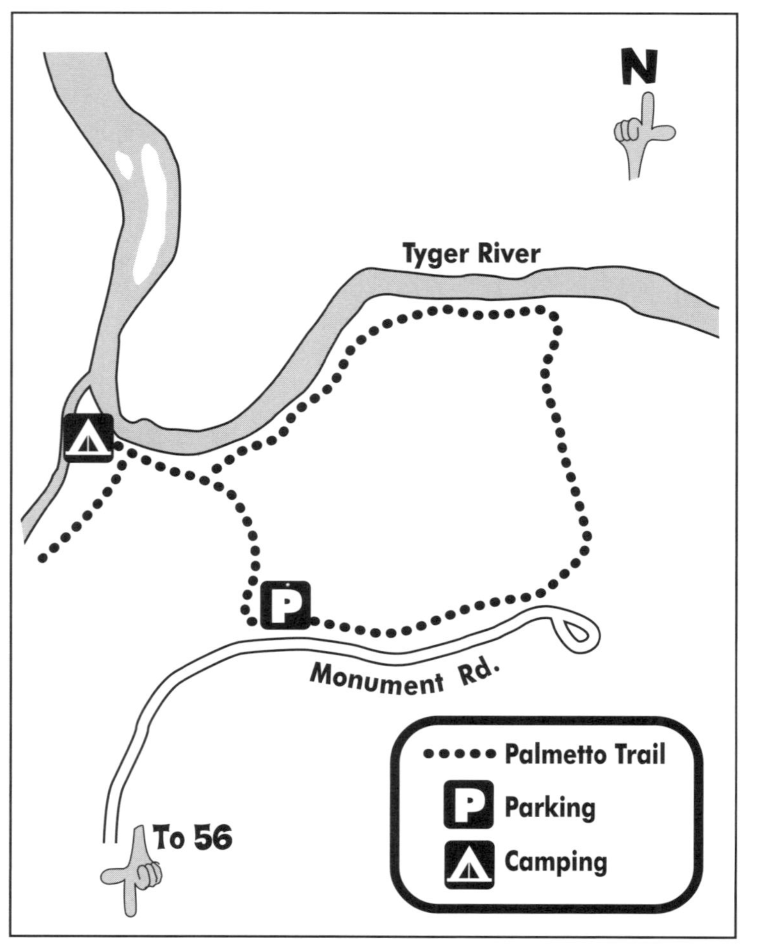
N
Tyger River
Monument Rd.
To 56
Palmetto Trail
Parking
Camping

Horseshoe Falls

Location: Musgrove Mill State Historic Site (Spartanburg County)
Directions: From Spartanburg, follow Interstate 26 east to exit 38 for SC 146. Follow SC 146 through Cross Anchor to where it becomes SC 56 and stay straight to Horseshoe Falls Road. Veer right and follow over an old bridge to one of two parking areas on the left. The second area is larger and offers a very short paved trail. From Musgrove Mill to Blackstock Battlefield, backtrack on SC 56 through Cross Anchor. Drive for 2.5 miles north of Cross Anchor to East Blackstock Road on the right (signs for Palmetto Trail trailhead). Turn right and follow 1 mile to Battlefield Road. Follow Battlefield Road 0.7-miles to a Y-intersection where you will veer left onto Monument Road. The Palmetto Trail trailhead is approximately one mile down on the left. You can stay straight to a cul de sac at the battlefield monument.
Hiking Time: N/A
Distance: There really is no hiking at Horseshoe Falls. Visit the nearby 1.5-mile Blackstock Battlefield Passage of the Palmetto Trail instead.
Difficulty level: Easy. Beware of slippery areas on the shoals.
Trail surface: The access is a mulched trail and the shoals are rocky.
Trail markings: N/A
Uses: Horseshoe Falls is a great swimming hole. Hiking, mountain biking, camping, birding and historical interpretation are available at nearby Blackstock Battlefield.
Facilities: None
Best time to visit: Summer is great at Horseshoe Falls, but winter is the best time to see the battlefield.
Dogs: Yes, on a leash.
Fees: None
Hours: Dawn to dusk
For more information:
Musgrove Mill State Historic Site
398 State Park Rd.
Clinton, SC 29325
(864) 938-0100
www.discvoersouthcarolina.com

Family Perk

The interpretive center at Musgrove Mill is a hub for the Cradle of Democracy project, a great educational destination for those interested about Revolutionary War history.

Photo by Michael Lowe.

Horseshoe Falls (aka Cedar Shoals Creek Swimming Hole) is just off the road, so you won't be able to do much hiking here. But this little-known area is a great family-friendly swimming hole during the summer (i.e. no alcohol or skinny dipping allowed) and great for paddling. Horseshoe Falls is just upstream of where Cedar Shoals Creek joins the Enoree River and a rocky area creates a series of cascades that drops about 10 feet and offers a nice pool at the base surrounded by a flat, sandy spot. The water is relatively shallow (3 feet or less), making it a great spot for children.

Musgrove Mill State Historic Site, which is on the Enoree River, is the first South Carolina State Park dedicated to the Revolutionary War and the state's first new park in more than a decade. Located at the juncture of Union, Laurens and Spartanburg counties, it features the remnants of Edward Musgrove's mill. A replica of his home that serves as a cozy visitor center and museum is the focal point of the 360-acre property. The 1,400 square-foot building features a fiber optic map of the grounds, along with audiovisual and three-dimensional exhibits that bring the 18th Century to life. One notable example is a display by the Daughters of the American Revolution, honoring women who accepted nontraditional roles such as spies and front-line soldiers.

Hiking options are available by making a 10-minute drive to a nearby 56-acre Revolutionary War battlefield that has been preserved for historical interpretation and now features hiking and mountain biking trails. The 1.5-mile Blackstock Battlefield Passage of the Palmetto Trail offers unforgettable views of the Tyger River from high bluffs overlooking this fantastic Piedmont forest. From the trailhead, the path loops east past the battlefield monument and soon descends gradually to the Tyger River where it hugs the riverbanks for a short distance. After passing through tunnels of mountain laurel, you can either double back to the parking area or follow to a primitive campsite on a creek that empties into the Tyger.

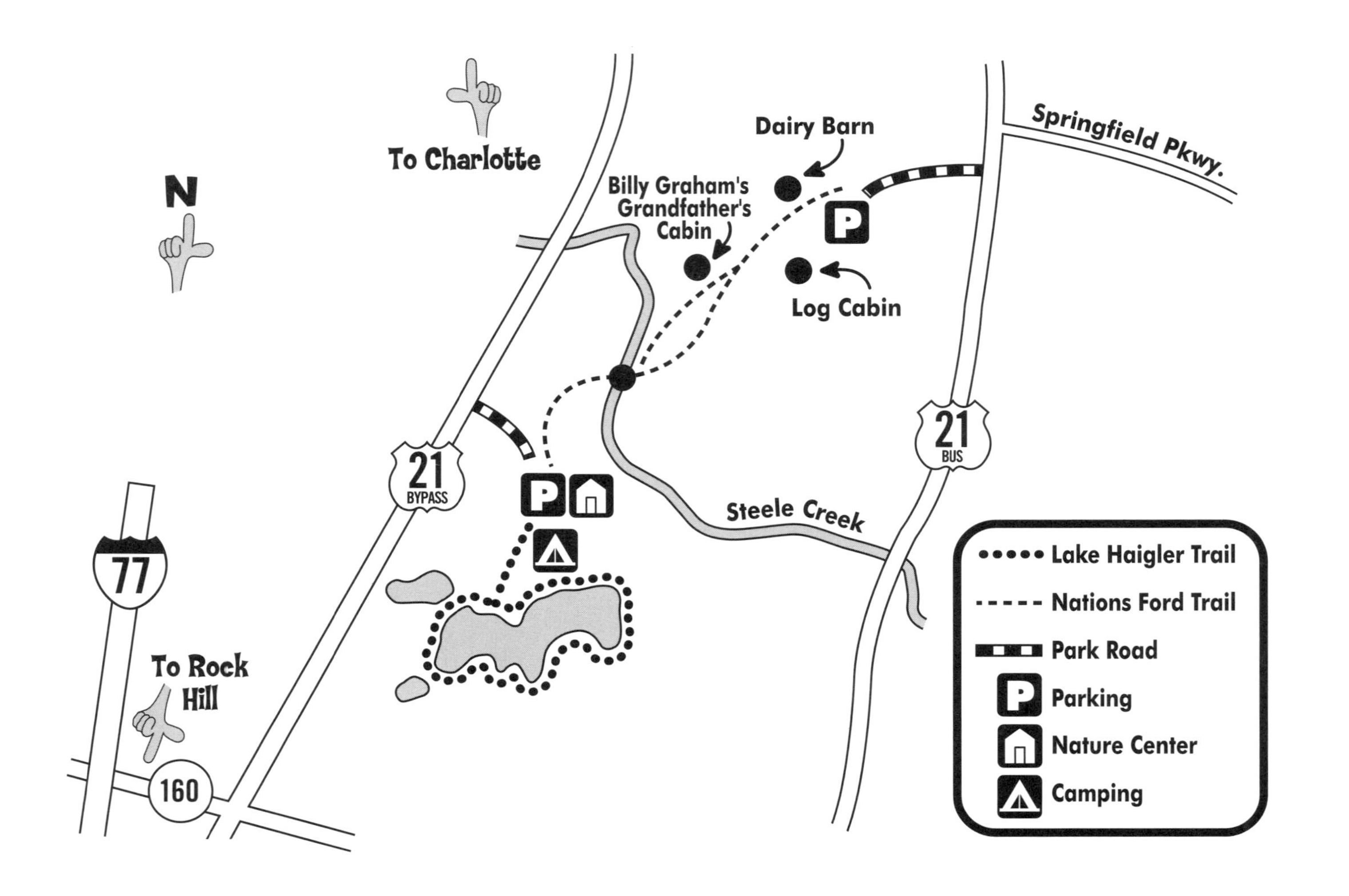

To Charlotte
N
Dairy Barn
Springfield Pkwy.
Billy Graham's
Grandfather's
Cabin
Log Cabin
21
BYPASS
21
BUS
Steele Creek
77
To Rock
Hill
160
Lake Haigler Trail
Nations Ford Trail
Park Road
Parking
Nature Center
Camping

Lake Haigler Trail

Location: Anne Springs Close Greenway (York County)
Directions: From Charlotte, travel south on Interstate 77 to Exit 85 for SC 160. Travel east toward Fort Mill crossing the US 21 bypass and continuing 0.7 mile to US 21 (business). Turn left and travel about 2.5 miles to the Dairy Barn entrance. Turn left onto the gravel road and follow to a parking lot and fee station on the left at 0.3 mile.
Hiking Time: 45 minutes
Distance: 1 mile loop (the Greenway includes more than 32 miles of multiple use trails).
Difficulty level: Easy
Trail surface: Natural dirt trail, some paved sidewalk (accessible for people with mobility impairments)
Trail markings: This trail is not marked although it is extremely easy to follow.
Uses: Hiking, biking, horseback riding, and fishing.
Facilities: Educational center, camping facilities, restrooms/showers located near the entrance to Lake Haigler and campsite.
Best time to visit: Spring is a fantastic time since the annual Earth Day celebration (mid April) is the biggest event each year, drawing more than 3,000 people.
Dogs: Yes, on a leash
Fees: Admission is free for members or $2 per person for hiking; $3 for bicycling, and $10 for primitive camping with bathhouse privileges (reservations are required). It is $10 per horse per day and fees apply for additional horses.
Hours: Open daily from 7 a.m. to sunset.
For more information:
Anne Springs Close Greenway
P.O. Box 1209
Fort Mill, SC 29716
(803) 548-7252
www.leroysprings.com

Family Perk

Guided horse trail rides are offered for youth nine years of age and older for a nominal cost. The rides take place from 4 to 5 p.m. Tuesdays and Fridays and from 10 to 11:30 a.m. on Saturdays. Pre-registration is required.

Photo courtesy s. jones ferguson.

With more than 32 miles of trails, children's learning programs and a popular Earth Day Celebration the Anne Springs Close Greenway has become arguably the best family-oriented nature preserve in the Piedmont and the easy, 1-mile Lake Haigler Trail is one of the best ways to experience it. Since opening in 1995, the 2,000-acre greenway has functioned as more of a park than a traditional, linear greenway. The land, which has been in the Close family for more than 200 years, was a gift to the citizens of Fort Mill by members of the Close family who sought to establish a buffer against urban encroachment.

Today, the greenway's hickory dogwood forests and 28-acre Lake Haigler form a graceful arc around the city of Fort Mill. The greenway is home to two barns for events and informal gatherings, a nature center, a historic log cabin and a bat house. Greenway staff often performs recreation and interpretive programs such as "Ecology Institute" and "History in a Backpack" programs for local school children.

The Lake Haigler trail begins at the nature center entrance and has 21 marked points of interest along the way, all of which are detailed in a brochure available at the nature center. The greenway also has an 8-foot-wide, 0.75-mile concrete surfaced trail that begins at the parking area and runs to an overlook on Steele Creek. In between, you will enjoy the renovated 1946 Dairy Barn, a log cabin dating back to the year 1800, a picturesque horse pasture, a log home built in 1780 that was once occupied by Billy Graham's grandfather.

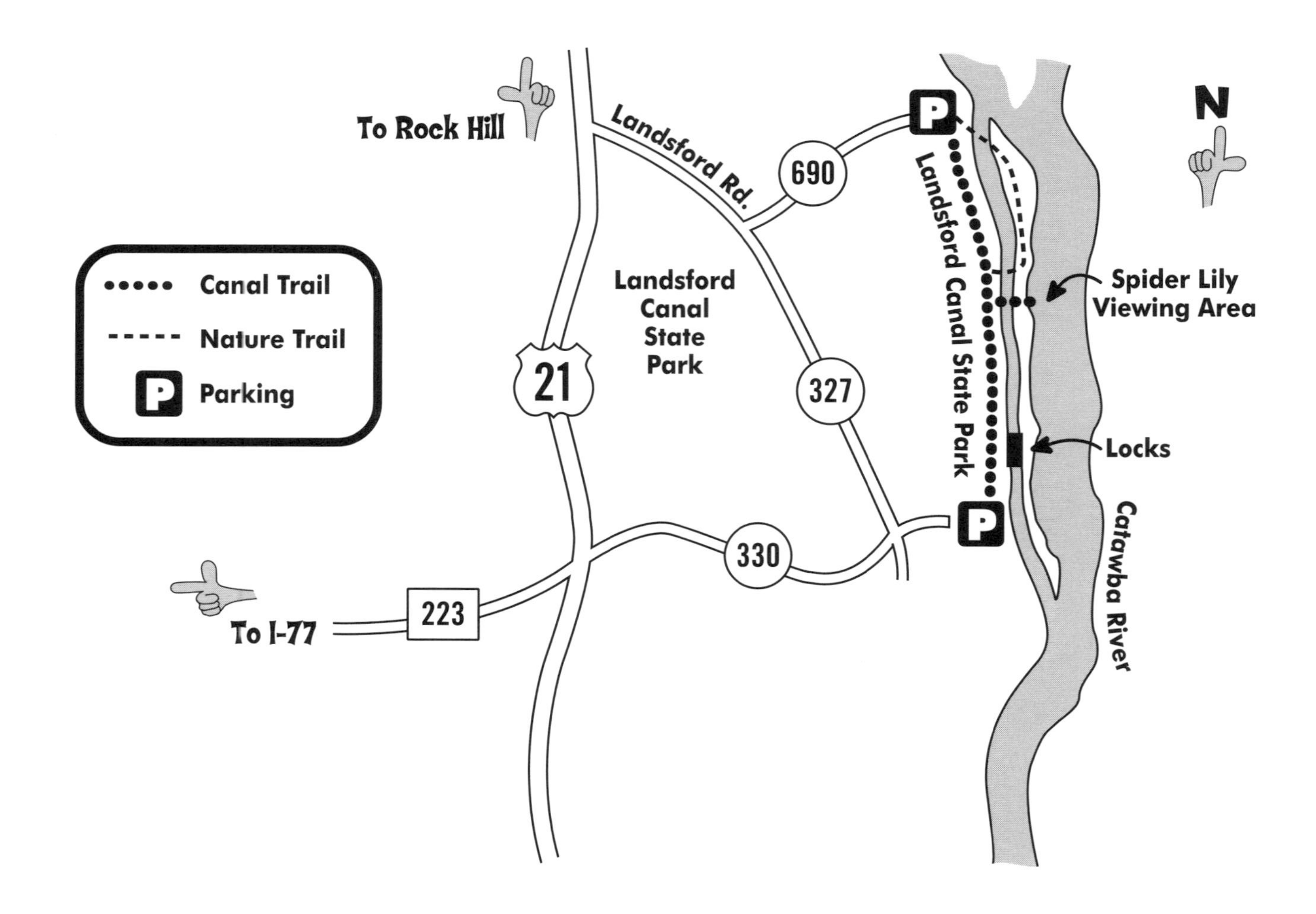

To Rock Hill
Landsford Rd.
690
N
Canal Trail
Nature Trail
Parking
Landsford Canal State Park
Landsford Canal State Park
Spider Lily Viewing Area
21
327
Locks
330
Catawba River
To I-77
223

Canal Trail

14

Location: Landsford Canal State Park (Chester County)
Directions: From Charlotte, travel south on Interstate 77. Take Exit 77 onto US 21 south (traveling away from Rock Hill) and drive for 10 miles until US 21 becomes a two-lane road. Turn left onto Landsford Road and drive two miles. The park entrance is on the left.
Hiking Time: One hour
Distance: 1.5 miles (one way)
Difficulty level: Easy
Trail surface: Natural surface, well defined tread with some moderate obstacles to those with mobility impairments but nothing difficult to negotiate. Can flood during periods of heavy rain.
Trail markings: The trail does not have blazes but is well-defined.
Uses: Hiking, birding and nature study.
Facilities: Restrooms and picnic tables are located near the parking area.
Best time to visit: Mid-May to mid-June - especially for the annual Lily Fest, a celebration of the world's largest colony of the Rocky Shoals spider Lily.
Dogs: Yes, on a leash
Fees: Admission is $2 per adult; $1.25 for seniors 65 and older and children ages 15 and younger are free.
Hours: Open Thursday through Monday from 9 a.m. to 6 p.m. Closed Tuesday and Wednesday.
For more information:
Landsford Canal State Park
2051 Park Dr.
Catawba, SC 29704
(803) 789-5800
www.discoversouthcarolina.com

Family Perk

Carolina Paddling Adventures offers guided trips on the Catawba River. Call (866) 858-0284.]

Photo courtesy s. jones ferguson.

Landsford Canal State Park is not well known outside of the Rock Hill/Chester area, but it should be. This park only has a few trails, including the easy, 1.5-mile Canal Trail, but the real reason to visit, from mid-May through June, is to see the world's largest colony of the Rocky Shoals Spider Lily blooming in a spectacular display that attracts floral enthusiasts from around the Southeast. Other natural wonders such as fall foliage and Lowcountry sunrises may get more attention in South Carolina, but Landsford Canal is one of a few places where you will hear grown men gasp at the sight of thousands of gangly, snow-white flowers drooping over the rushing Catawba River.

Although the Canal Trail is enjoyable anytime of year, it is best during the spider lily display when families can visit the park, set up in the picnic area and then gaze over the Catawba River at the lilys or launch out for some exploring. Paddling is a very popular pastime here (a great paddling trail begins at the park) and many families fish for bass, crappie, bream and catfish from the riverbanks. The Canal Trail begins from the main parking area and runs along the historic towpath of the canal eventually passing the foundation of a mill (circa 1800).The surroundings are a mature riparian forest of tall oak, sweetgum, hickory and river birch.

Birding enthusiasts can usually find something here year-round, although the best seasons are spring and fall. The species to look for include bald eagles, prothonotary warblers (April through August), migrant warblers (April–May and September–October) and scarlet tanagers (mid-April through October).

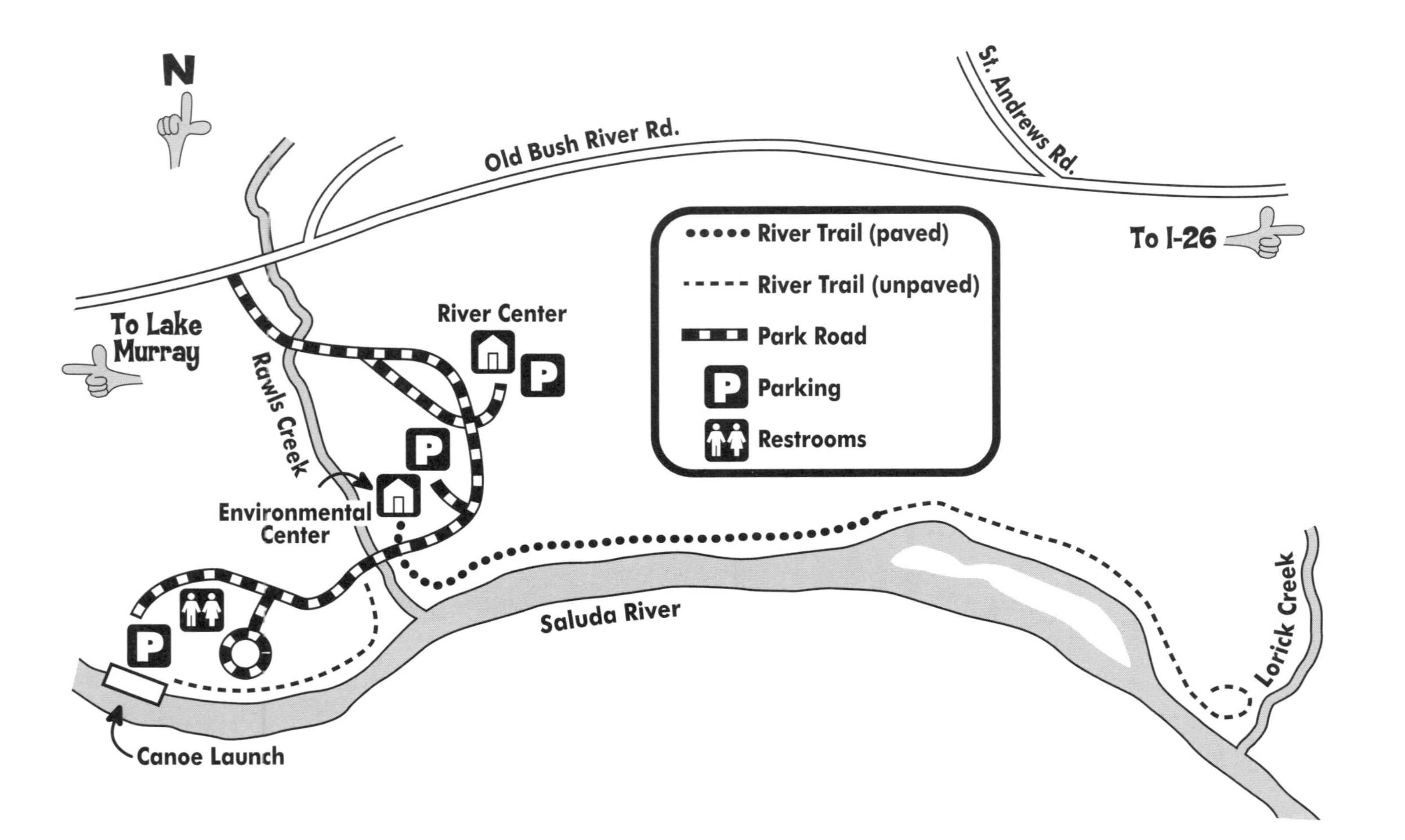

N
Old Bush River Rd.
St. Andrews Rd.
To I-26
To Lake Murray
River Trail (paved)
River Trail (unpaved)
Park Road
Parking
Restrooms
River Center
Rawls Creek
Environmental Center
Saluda River
Lorick Creek
Canoe Launch

Saluda Shoals Park

Location: Saluda Shoals Park (Lexington County)
Directions: From Columbia, drive northwest on I-26 to Exit 104. Turn left onto Piney Grove Road. Follow Piney Grove approximately 1.5 miles to St. Andrews Road. Turn right, then left at the first traffic light onto Bush River Road. The park entrance is 1.5 miles on the left. Enter the park and after you cross a bridge you will see the fee station. Continue to the Environmental Center, which is on the right, or continue to the end of the road to the canoe launch area.
Hiking Time: varies
Distance: 4 to 5 miles of interconnecting trails
Difficulty level: Easy. Nature trails are muddy after the rain and have numerous roots and obstacles that would be difficult for very young children and older hikers.
Trail surface: Paved and natural surface trails, some dirt and boardwalks.
Trail markings: The trails are not marked, however they are very easy to follow.
Uses: Walking, running, hiking, horseback riding (pre-registration required), mountain biking, canoeing/kayaking, fishing, bird watching, water playground, picnics/outdoor gatherings.
Facilities: Environmental Center (educational exhibits in natural history) has drink machines, River Center (meeting/event venue), picnic shelters, boat ramp/canoe/kayak launch. Public restroom facilities are located in the Environmental Center and at the Saluda Splash Park.
Best time to visit: The spring and summer months are when most of the special activities at the park are scheduled.
Dogs: Yes, on a leash.
Fees: $4 per car (annual pass available).
Hours: 7 a.m. to 8 p.m.
For more information:
Saluda Shoals Park
5605 Bush River Road
Columbia, SC 29212
(803) 731-5208
www.icrc.net

Family Perk

Throughout the spring and summer months the park offers numerous activities ranging from outdoor evening movies, day camps, guided canoe day-trips and weeklong horseback riding camps.

The Saluda Shoals Park in Irmo offers a wide range of activities that are appealing to both parents and kids of all ages - especially its excellent 4- to 5-mile network of both hard surface and unpaved nature trails. Located along the Saluda River southeast of Lake Murray, the park covers 300 acres of both wooded and open space perfect for a family day trip. Visitors have a choice between hiking or biking down paved, open trails, or veering off into the woods on the property's nature trails where birds and other wildlife are abundant. After a morning of hiking on the property, visitors can cool off in the Environmental Center where they can view displays on the area's natural history or buy a cool drink and souvenir at the gift shop.

Photo by Jennifer Revels

The newly opened Saluda Splash water playground is a fun way for the kids to cool off, and the whole family will enjoy a trip down the Saluda River in a canoe or kayak available for rental at the boat launch. Stay late two Fridays a month for Cinema in the Park, where family-friendly movies play outdoors on the big screen right by the river!

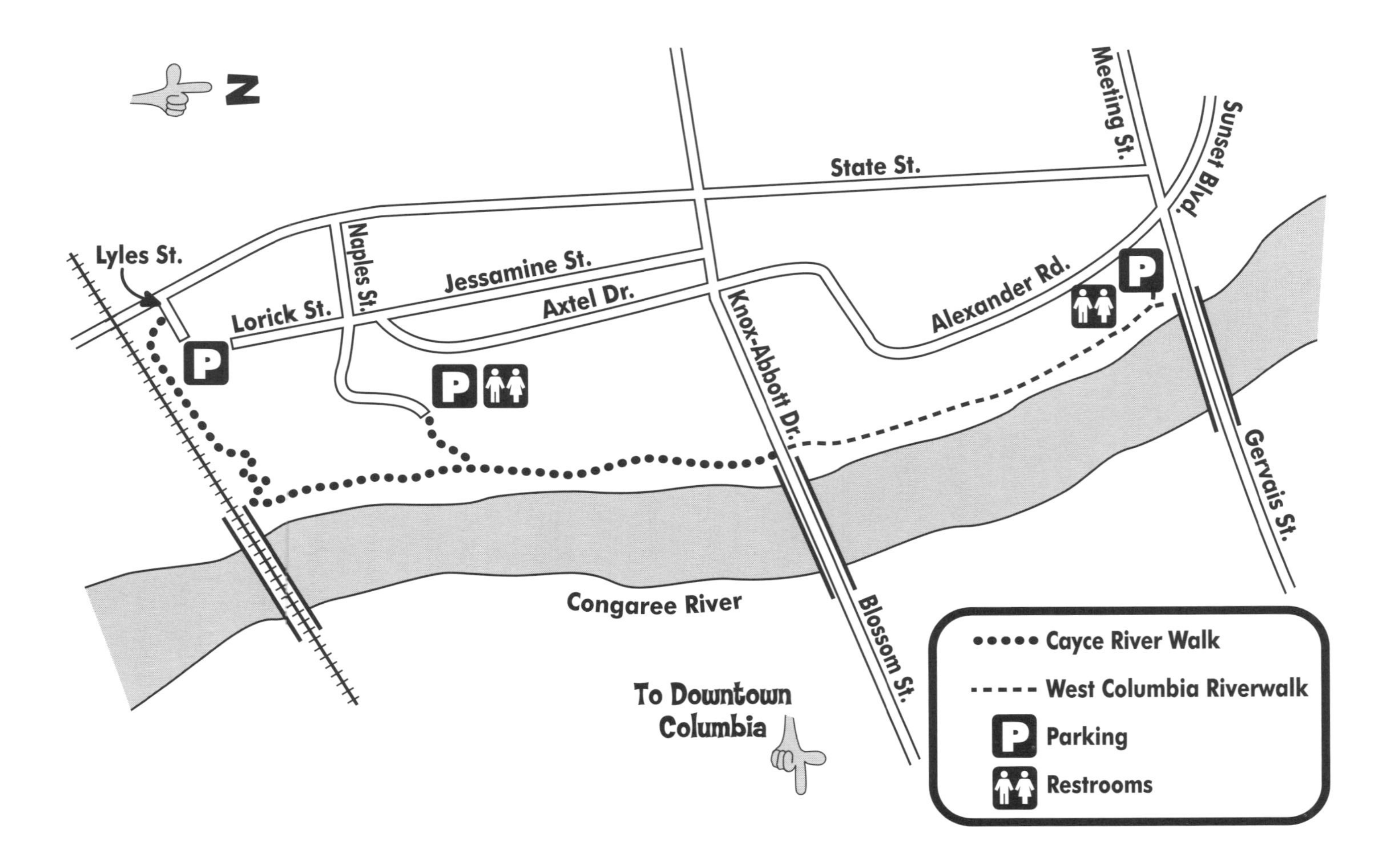

N
Lyles St.
Lorick St.
Naples St.
Jessamine St.
Axtel Dr.
State St.
Knox-Abbott Dr.
Alexander Rd.
Meeting St.
Sunset Blvd.
Gervais St.
Congaree River
Blossom St.
To Downtown Columbia
Cayce River Walk
West Columbia Riverwalk
Parking
Restrooms

Three Rivers Greenway

Location: Cayce, across the Congaree River from Columbia (Richland County)
Directions: The West Columbia Riverwalk trailhead: Cross the Gervais Street Bridge from Columbia, take first left onto Alexander Road. The parking area is immediately to the left. This parking area is ADA-friendly with ample handicap parking spaces and ramps to the trail.
The Cayce Riverwalk trailhead: Take the Blossom Street Bridge from Columbia to Knox-Abbott Drive in Cayce. Take a left at the first traffic light onto Axtell Drive. Continue until Axtell becomes Jessamine Street; parking area is immediately to the left. The parking lot is gravel, however, two spaces are paved at the trailhead for ADA access.
The southern trailhead: Take the Blossom Street Bridge from Columbia to Knox-Abbott Drive in Cayce. Take a left at the first traffic light onto Axtell Drive. Continue until Axtell becomes Jessamine Street; continue straight, parking area is at the road's end. This is not a formal parking area and there is no ADA accessibility.
Granby Park trailhead: From I-126, take Huger Street cross Blossom Street and take a right onto Catawba Street.
Hiking Time: 1 hour round trip
Distance: approximately 3 miles (round trip)
Difficulty level: Easy
Trail surface: Paved pathway, natural trail and some bridges/boardwalk. Signs at the beginning of the trail warn about the surface becoming slick after heavy rain.
Trail markings: The main path is well marked with wooden post signs.
Uses: Hiking, biking/mountain biking, skating/skateboarding, fishing, canoe/kayak access
Facilities: Picnic areas and benches (with garbage cans) are scattered along the trail, restrooms are located at the West Columbia and Cayce Riverwalk parking areas with ADA accessible facilities and baby changing stations. Emergency call boxes are also located in the parking areas and along the trail every half mile. Granby Park has a parking area with restrooms.
Best time to visit: The majority of the trail is shaded; however, the close proximity to the river produces a great deal of humidity in the summer. Spring and fall are the best times to walk the trail because limited tree cover provides a greater view of the Congaree River and the Columbia skyline.
Dogs: Yes, on a leash. Clean-up bags are provided at the parking areas.
Fees: None
Hours: Open daily during daylight hours only. Lighting along the trail provides light during dawn and dusk.
For more information: River Alliance
506 Gervais Street
Columbia, SC 29201
(803) 765-2200
www.riveralliance.org

Family Perk

Through the spring and early summer months the facility's amphitheater hosts a weekly concert series called Rhythm on the River. There are also educational kiosks throughout the trail that discuss Columbia history and animals that are common to the area.

Photo by Jennifer Revels

The Three Rivers Greenway is a newly created recreational trail tucked away along the Congaree River in Columbia. Conveniently located in downtown Columbia minutes from the South Carolina State Museum and EdVenture Children's Museum, the 1.5 mile trail combines education and entertainment within a natural atmosphere and is an easy hike for young children as well as older adults. As you walk the length of the greenway, birds and small animals can be heard above the ever-present gurgle of the Congaree River. A closer look at the river may reveal a turtle sunning on a log or a gray heron in search of food. For nature lovers, kiosks show photos of plants and animals that can be observed throughout the hike. These small kiosks also talk about the history of Columbia, the geology of the river and how it was formed.

The Greenway parallels the Congaree River across from the city of Columbia, affording breathtaking views of both the river and the skyline of South Carolina's capital city. The main trail is mostly shaded and paved to allow for roller blading as well as baby strollers and wheelchairs. There are ample resting areas with picnic tables and benches that overlook the river. The greenway also includes a dirt path for mountain bikes that runs in a 2-mile loop through the dense woods along the main path. Across the Congaree at Granby Park, there is a second 1-mile walking trail and 1.5-mile mountain biking trail with access to the river for canoeing and kayaking.

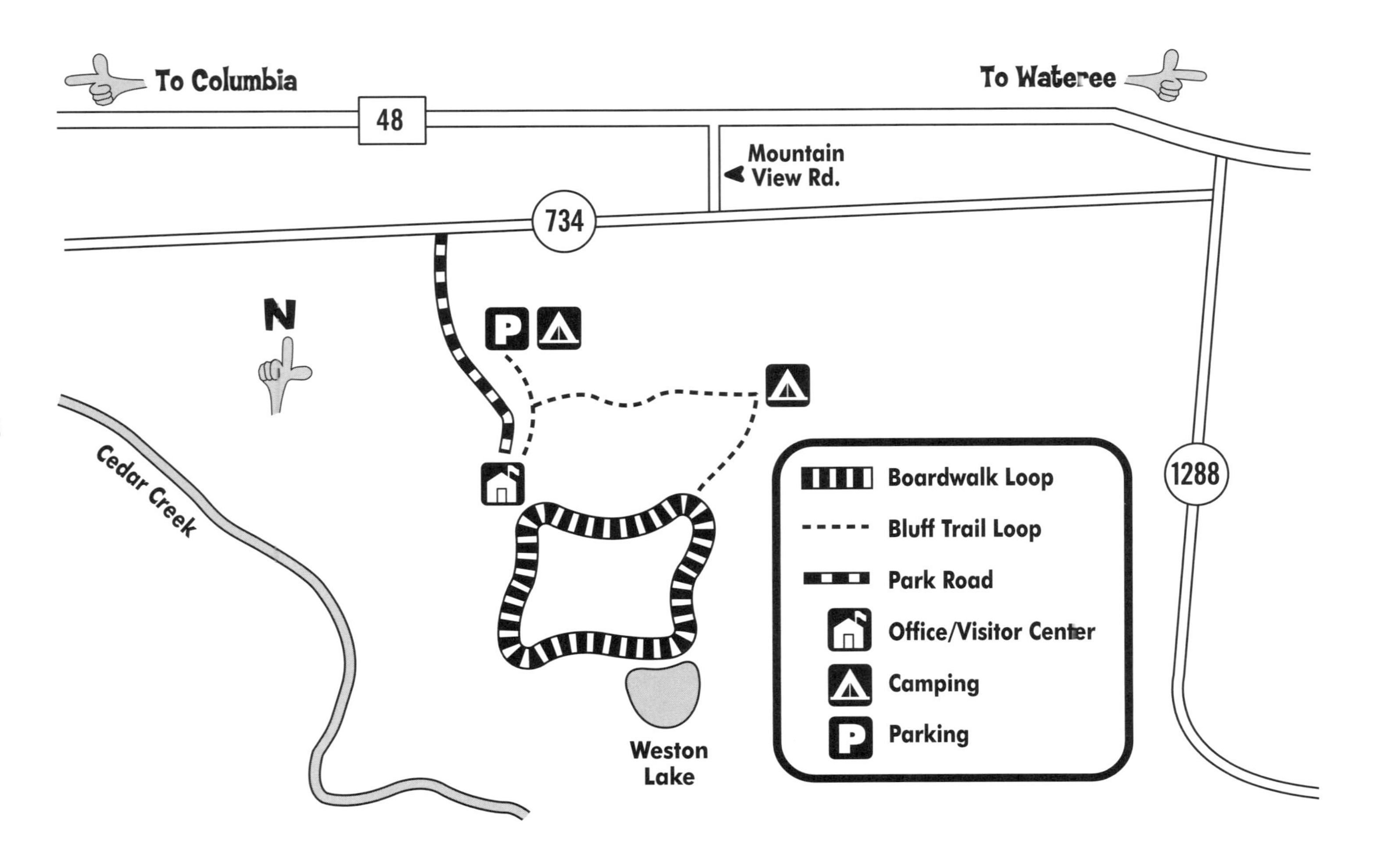
To Columbia
To Wateree
48
Mountain
View Rd.
734
N
1288
Cedar Creek
Boardwalk Loop
Bluff Trail Loop
Park Road
Office/Visitor Center
Camping
Parking
P
Weston
Lake

Boardwalk Loop, Congaree National Park

Location: Congaree National Park (Richland County)
Directions: From Columbia, follow Interstate 77 to exit 5 for Bluff Road (SC 48). (Watch for brown and white "Congaree Swamp National Monument" directional signs to the park.) Travel southeast for 12 miles on SC 48 to a right turn onto Mt. View Rd. Travel 0.8 miles to the end of the road and turn right onto Old Bluff Road and travel 0.4 miles to the park entrance. Turn left onto the park entrance road and travel 1.2 miles to the Harry Hampton Visitor Center.
Hiking Time: About 1.5 hours
Distance: 2.4 mile loop
Difficulty level: Easy
Trail surface: Boardwalk (accessible for people with mobility impairments)
Trail markings: Well marked. Other trails in the park are blazed in yellow, red, blue, white and orange.
Uses: Hiking, birding, fishing, camping, canoeing, and kayaking.
Facilities: Harry Hampton Visitor Center is accessible for those with mobility impairments and includes restrooms and a picnic area. There is a soft drink machine and exhibits at the visitor center.
Best time to visit: Special programs are offered during spring and fall. Children will love the Owl Prowls, which take place in spring and fall.
Dogs: Allowed in the park (on a leash) but not on the Boardwalk Loop Trail.
Fees: None (There is no entrance fee at Congaree National Park).
Hours: Dawn to dusk. Closed Christmas Day.
For more information:
Congaree National Park
100 National park Rd.
Hopkins, SC 29061
(803) 776-4396
www.nps.gov/cosw

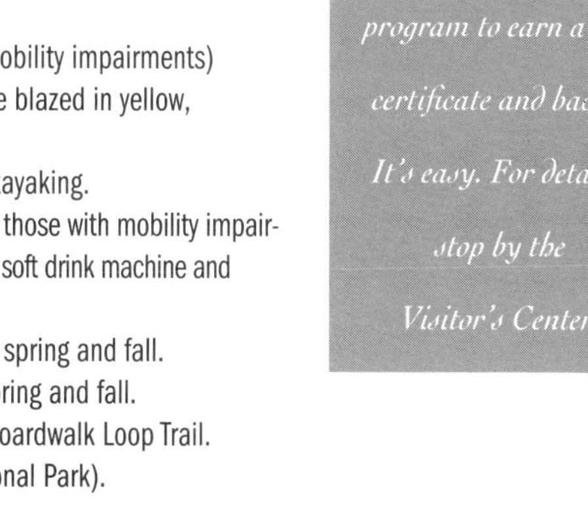

Family Perk

Children may complete the Junior Ranger program to earn a free certificate and badge. It's easy. For details, stop by the Visitor's Center.

The easy, 2.4-mile Boardwalk Loop at Congaree National Park is one of the most unique trails in this guide - perhaps in the Southeast. Beginning from the Harry Hampton Visitor Center, this trail meanders out into this phenomenal 22,000-acre park, passing through dense bottomland hardwood forests. The boardwalk is raised off the ground and provides visitors with an easy path for viewing a variety of animal and plant life. Along the way hikers should listen for the distinctive sound of woodpeckers in the trees above and also try to spot some of the more than 150 trees that measure more than 12 feet in circumference. In the warmer months families should be sure to bring insect repellent and protective clothing as biting insects can thwart any outing. Maps and brochures are available in the Visitors Center to help families in planning other hiking routes. Adventurous families may opt to take advantage of the park's canoe and kayak trails used for navigating the area's dynamic floodplain wilderness. Although no canoe or kayak rentals are available in the park, several outfitters are available in nearby Columbia. As a precaution paddlers should call the Visitors Center (number listed above) for conditions before beginning any trip.

Photo by Oliver Buckles.

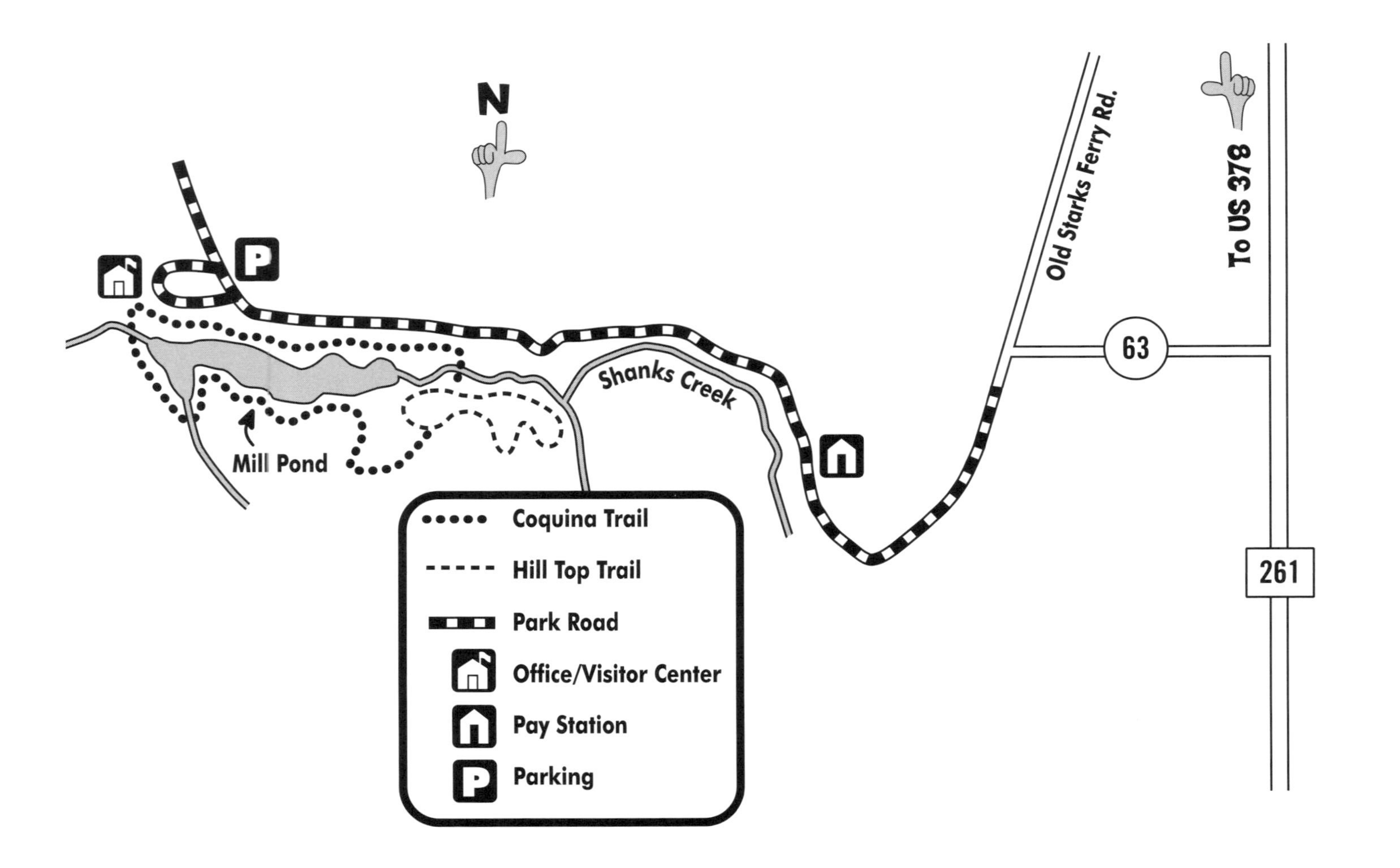

N
Old Starks Ferry Rd.
To US 378
63
261
Shanks Creek
Mill Pond
Coquina Trail
Hill Top Trail
Park Road
Office/Visitor Center
Pay Station
Parking

Coquina Nature Trail

18

Location: Poinsett State Park near Sumter (Sumter County)
Directions: From Columbia, drive east (west from Sumter) on US 378 and turn south onto SC 261. Drive for 10 miles and turn right onto Park Road (Sumter County S-43-63) and drive approximately 1.9 miles to Poinsett State Park and the trailhead is at the end of the road by the park office.
Hiking Time: One hour
Distance: 1.5 miles (one way)
Difficulty level: Easy to moderate
Trail surface: Natural, hard packed dirt and sandy loam. Some rolling terrain.
Trail markings: The trail is the park's most popular and is very well-marked.
Uses: Hiking and birding. Other trails in the area allow mountain biking.
Facilities: Restrooms and drinking water are available at the parking area. The park also has more than 50 campsites, vacation cabins, picnic areas and a lake for fishing.
Best time to visit: Late fall is definitely the best time of year here since clear skies can offer unforgettable views and the autumn colors are tremendous.
Dogs: Yes, on a leash.
Fees: $2 per adult; $1.25 for seniors. Children 15 and under are free.
Hours: Open daily from 9 a.m. to 6 p.m. (hours extended to 9 p.m. on Friday, Saturday and Sunday in Daylight Savings Time.)
For more information:
Poinsett State Park
6660 Poinsett Park Road
Wedgefield, SC 29168
(803) 494-8177
www.discoversouthcarolina.com

Family Perk

Children under 15 are free.

Photo by Oliver Buckles.

Coquina (pronounced ko-ke-na) is a soft, porous limestone, which is composed essentially of fragments of shells and coral. It's a fine name for a trail - and you'll see some of the stone along the way - but in reality the easy, 1.5-mile Coquina Nature Trail is misnamed. The trail passes through a hilly, 1,000-acre park in Sumter County that was probably once covered by ocean water and today, despite the flatness of the surrounding landscape, has all the trappings of a Piedmont hillside. It's probably one of the few places in the world where mountain laurel grows beneath a veil of Spanish moss. The park is home to galax, oaks, dogwood, pine and more than 50 bird species.

From a parking area near the campground, the trail meanders past the western tip of Mill Pond and climbs up a 100-foot bluff to a rain shelter with great views of the pond below. The trail eventually joins the Hilltop Trail, which is short but requires a good bit of climbing. If you continue on the Coquina Trail, you will eventually drop back down to circle the other side of Mill Pond and cross a boardwalk in a beautiful swamp. Other sections of trail in the area include the High Hills Passage of the Palmetto Trail which overlays some existing trail and eventually leaves the park boundary and travels into nearby Manchester State Forest. This 14-mile passage which ends at Mill Creek County Park is more than a day hike - and probably not doable for families - but day hiking is possible in Poinsett State Park.

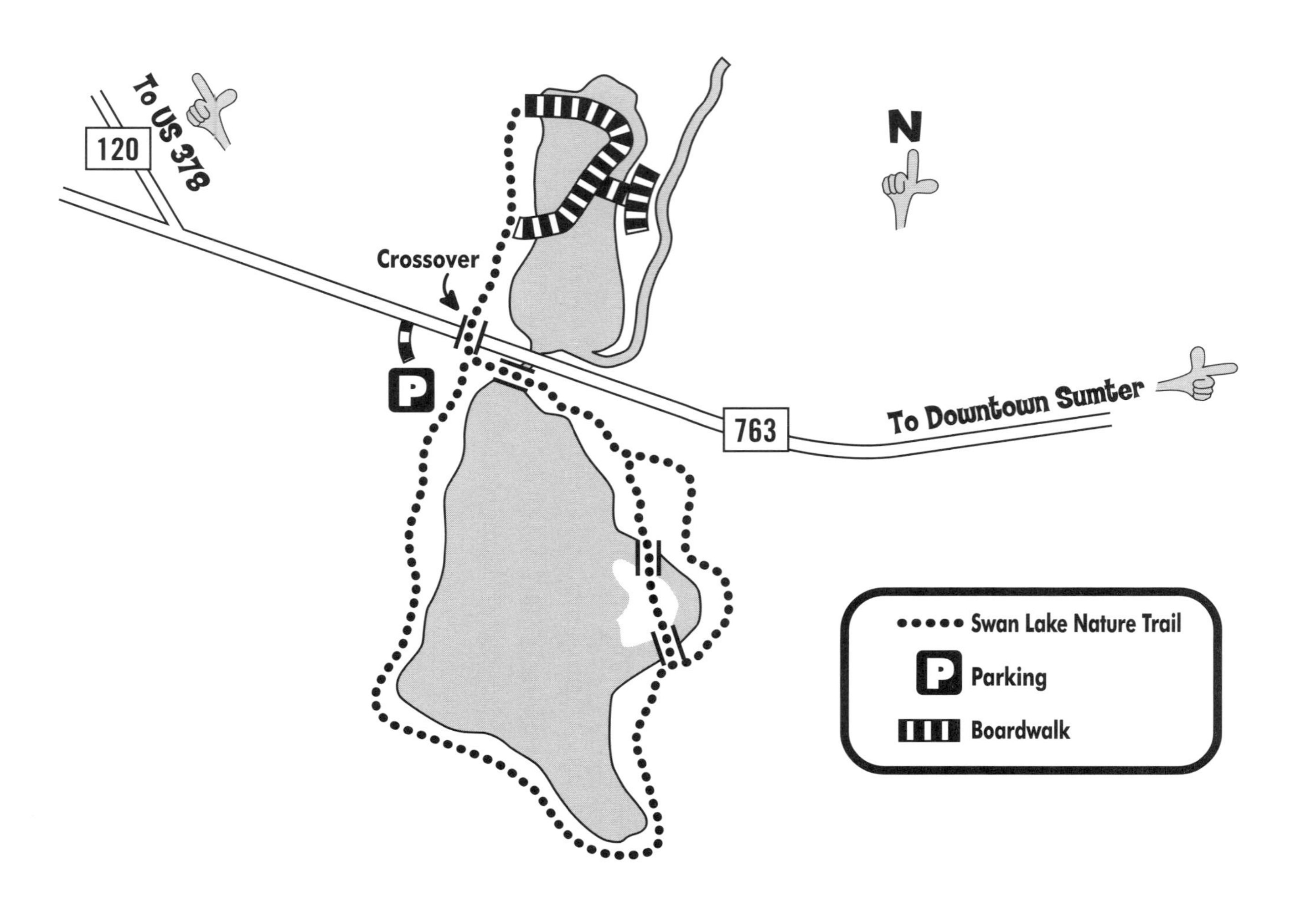
To US 378
120
N
Crossover
P
763
To Downtown Sumter
Swan Lake Nature Trail
Parking
Boardwalk

Swan Lake Trails

Location: Swan Lake-Iris Garden (Sumter County)
Directions: From Columbia, follow US 76/378 to Sumter and turn right (south) onto Alice Drive (SC 120). Follow Alice Drive for 2.5 miles to West Liberty St. (SC 763). Turn left and continue a very short distance to the Swan Lake entrance on the right.
Hiking Time: One hour
Distance: 1.5 mile (loop)
Difficulty level: Easy
Trail surface: Natural, sandy and grass paths with boardwalks and an overpass across the highway.
Trail markings: Trails are well maintained with many markers explaining the history of the gardens.
Uses: Hiking, birding and wildlife viewing.
Facilities: Restrooms and drinking water are available at the parking area and at several places in the park. The garden also includes a "Braille trail" and is accessible to those with mobility impairments.
Best time to visit: Spring (late May) is best because of the annual Sumter Iris Festival each Memorial Day Weekend, which has been happening since the 1940s. There are more than 6 million Japanese Iris blossoms here - more than any place in the nation.
Dogs: Yes, on a leash.
Fees: Free
Hours: Dawn to dusk
For more information:
City of Sumter/Swan Lake-Iris Gardens
West Liberty St.
(800) 688-4748
www.sumter-sc.com

Family Perk

In addition to the Iris Festival, a "Fantasy of Lights" display is popular during the Christmas season. Don't forget to let your children feed the swans!

Photo by Oliver Buckles.

South Carolina has many well-loved city parks that are popular with locals but rarely draw visitors from afar. Swan Lake-Iris Gardens - the only place in the world with all eight known species of swans, a stunning display of Japanese Irises and accessible trail system - is one of those parks. With two gardens connected via a pedestrian overpass across Liberty Street (the smaller 30-acre Bland Garden is on the north side of the road while the 120-acre Heath Garden is on the south side), both properties feature different and equally appealing assets made possible by Swan Lake.

The main parking area is on the south side of Liberty Street and allows easy access to the spacious Heath Garden. From the parking area, there is easy access to a pavilion, concession stand and restrooms as well as a playground with an old fire engine (great for climbing). The trail loops around Swan Lake for almost three-quarters of a mile and passes thick beds of irises, cypress trees and many benches that enable visitors to stretch out and enjoy the scenery. The lake has a number of islands that provide a refuge for the swans that are fiercely protective of their territory in mating season and must be separated to keep them from fighting. If you have children with you, make sure to stop off at a grazing area adopted by the swans.

On the north side of Liberty Street, the lake features an earthen dam with wild cypress swamps beyond. On this side of the lake, look for "swandominiums" where baby swans are raised and some protected nesting areas. The Bland Garden is far more intimate than the south side of the lake since one path leads past a gazebo to shady islands and a wooden walkway leads into the depths of the swamp. Make sure you stop off at the swan feeders and remember to wear insect repellant in warmer weather.

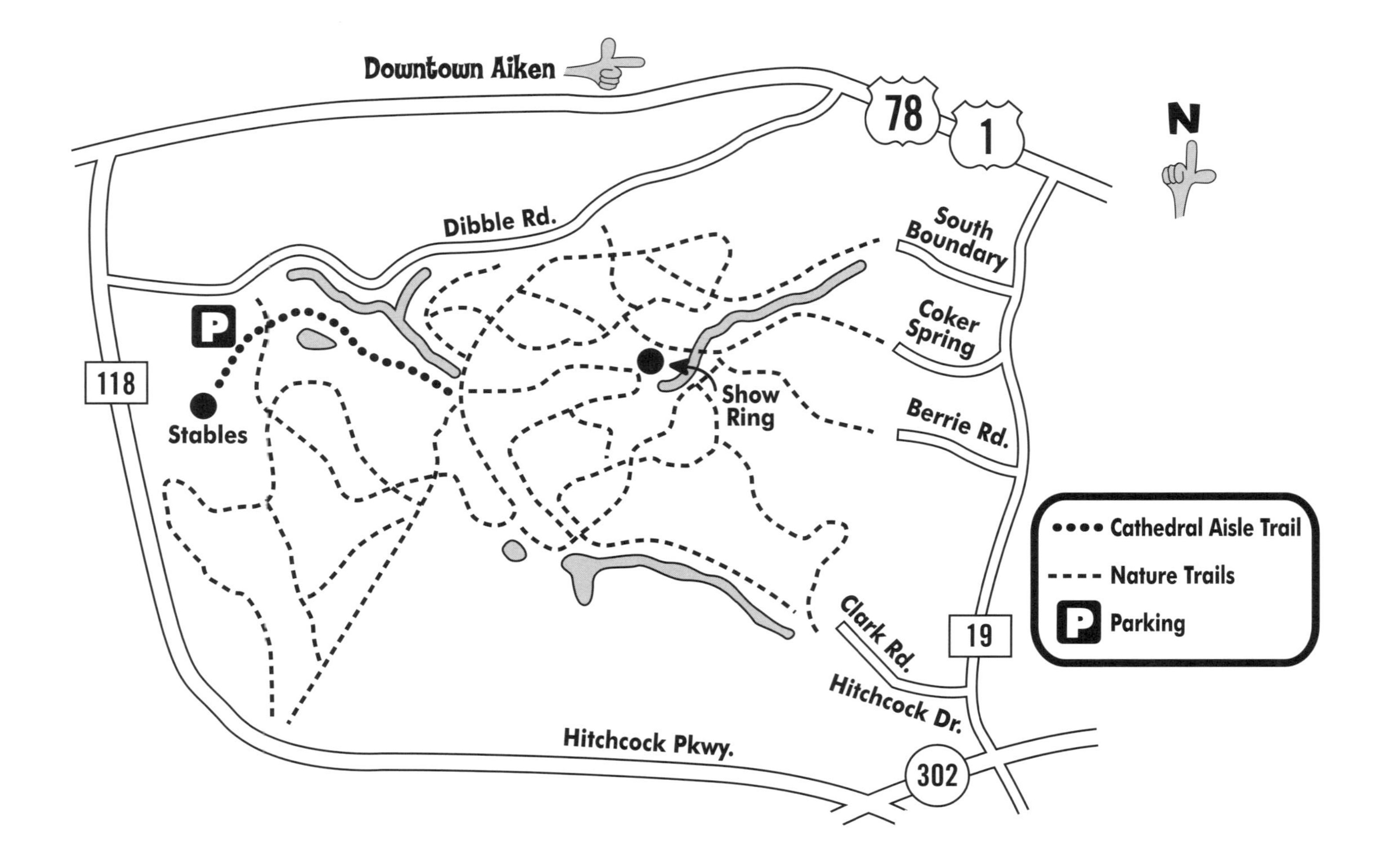
Downtown Aiken
78
1
N
Dibble Rd.
South Boundary
Coker Spring
Show Ring
Berrie Rd.
118
Stables
Cathedral Aisle Trail
Nature Trails
Parking
19
Clark Rd.
Hitchcock Dr.
Hitchcock Pkwy.
302

Cathedral Aisle Trail

Location: Hitchcock Woods in Aiken (Aiken County)
Directions: From US 1/SC 118 in Aiken, turn left onto Dibble Road, Travel past SCE&G natural gas station and follow signs for Fulmer International. At the entrance to the woods, you'll see a map box. Cathedral Aisle is straight ahead.
Hiking Time: 0.5 to 1.5 hours
Distance: 1 mile
Difficulty level: Easy
Trail surface: Natural surface, primarily sandy roadbeds and narrow footpaths. Some hills, but the trails are mainly flat.
Trail markings: Trails are all well signed, but we strongly recommend bringing a map. The trails crisscross frequently and some spur trails are dead ends. Stop by a map box on your way in.
Uses: Hiking, horseback riding.
Facilities: No camping.
Best time to visit: Spring, especially March and April. In March, horseracing events such as the Triple Crown draw many visitors and the azaleas are amazing.
Dogs: Yes, on a leash.
Fees: None
Hours: Dawn to dusk
For more information:
Hitchcock Woods
PO Box 1702
Aiken, SC 29802
(803) 642-0528
www.hitchcockwoods.org

Family Perk

The nearby Silver Bluff Center and Sanctuary is a wonderful site for nature and environmental study operated by the National Audubon Society.

Photo by Michael Lowe.

It is all but impossible to tell families to focus on one single trail in the 2,100-acre Hitchcock Woods, which many say is the largest urban park in the United States. (Central Park in New York City, by the way, is a paltry 843 acres). Those who know this area well can jog past sand "rivers," chalky cliffs, blooming mountain laurel and Spanish moss in one trip. But the 1-mile, easy roadbed that comprises the initial part of the Cathedral Aisle Trail is a great place to start since it's a great surface for kids (or baby strollers), takes off from the most popular of the Woods' seven parking areas and provides access to the heart of the forest.

Focusing on one trail here is difficult since more than 50 miles of paths in Hitchcock Woods often double back on themselves, suddenly sprout new names and occasionally even disappear into shady pine forest groves. But because the turns are well marked, it's actually easy to explore, especially when you start on the Cathedral Aisle Trail. This trail, which may be the first "rails-to-trails" conversion in the entire country, is part of a railroad line that was built in 1833 by the S.C. Canal & Railroad Company to run from Hamburg to Charleston. The railbed was abandoned in the early 1850s and this portion is now a lovely trail. The Hitchcock Foundation was established in 1939 through the generosity of Thomas Hitchcock and his daughter, Helen Clark. They donated approximately 1,200 acres of land for the recreational use and enjoyment by the people of Aiken. The Hitchcock Foundation, a non-profit organization, is managed by a board of trustees and is dependent upon the private support of those who value and treasure this unique natural resource. If you choose to explore off the Cathedral Aisle Trail, a few areas that beg for a visit include Sand River, Ridge Mile Track, Tea Cottage and Kalmia Trail (a shor distance easy of Cathedral Aisle Trail). This last follows a ridge that blooms in mountain laurel (aka Kalmia) during March and April. Tea cottage is the site of a cottage built by Mrs. Thomas Hitchcock's aunt, Miss Celestine Eustis. The cottage was used as a place for entertainment until it was lost to fire in the 1970s. Ridge Mile Track was built by Thomas Hitchcock to train his racehorses in the 1920s and 1930s.

Lowcountry

Text by Amanda Capps

More often than not, families journey to the Lowcountry with visions of relaxing days at a familiar beach house. Many others certainly look forward to romping on the sand at Hilton Head or cavorting through the famous Myrtle Beach Pavilion. To Palmetto State visitors (and even some longtime residents), the surrounding swamps, sprawling marshes and buggy forests can seem uninviting or even unpleasant - certainly not places that parents would want to bring young children for a morning walk. But, in truth, the Lowcountry is a delightful place to live or visit for a family that enjoys outdoor activities such as walking, birding or jogging.

For instance, in the Pee Dee, where cotton and tobacco once ruled, blackwater rivers now roll lazily toward a glitzy coastline that is among the most developed anywhere in the world. But nearby, the southern beaches and towns of South Carolina's Grand Strand are subtler than their glamorous neighbors. Sandy Island offers a natural refuge that also happens to be the largest undeveloped freshwater island in the East. In the Charleston area, a top-flight county parks and recreation system provides excellent family-oriented destinations that offer everything from the simple pleasures of a wooded hiking trail to a towering climbing wall. One of our destinations is also a privately developed community built on scale for walkers that performs extensive outreach to its residents and visitors to get people walking and bicycling.

In the southernmost portion of South Carolina, Beaufort, Port Royal, Bluffton and Hilton Head Island offer some of the finest beaches in the country - with many family-friendly outdoor activities included. Beaufort County, in particular, is becoming a haven for walkers and bicyclists, with Hilton Head Island leading the way by adding miles of new paths and trails.

Note! *While there are many family friendly opportunities available throughout the Lowcountry, it is important to remember that we focused on just a few areas close to the trails in this book. Make sure that you do plenty of exploring too!*

Detours *No family-oriented hiking trip is complete without stopping off either en route or on the way home for ice cream, folksy stories, good food or educational opportunities. Here are just a few family-oriented locations in the Lowcountry and near our favorite family walking trails.*

Horry and Georgetown Counties

(For hikes #21 and 22: Little Bull Creek Trail and Sandpiper Pond Trail)

Although the entire area from Pawley's Island to Cherry Grove is commonly called Myrtle Beach, the actual beach sits in the middle of a 60-mile stretch of hallowed vacationland known as the Grand Strand. And for years, the center of it all has been the Myrtle Beach Pavilion - a hub for vacationers of all ages. Generations of South Carolinians recall nights under the Pavilion's lights in the heart of "The Strip," and whether you are on foot, in a convertible or on a motorcycle, cruising is the activity of choice. However, there are plenty of other choices including clubs, museums and endless venues for outfitting any beach bum. The Pavilion is on 9th Avenue between Ocean Boulevard and US 17. If you take the family, be sure to stay for your money's worth, as admission is $23.95 plus tax for adults and $14.95 plus tax for seniors and children.

Farther up US 17 near North Myrtle Beach, Broadway at the Beach and Barefoot Landing combine stores, restaurants, and theaters in today's more aesthetic answer to the shopping mall. Ripley's Aquarium is one of the stars on Broadway. A past winner of the Governor's Cup for Tourism, Ripley's redefines expectations of theme parks. Interactive computer stations allow children to ask their own questions. Amazing exhibits take guests on tours of the Bermuda Triangle and the Amazon. But, the real showcase is a 330-foot moving walkway designed to simulate underwater diving. Twelve-foot sharks swim overhead as visitors take this unique journey. Broadway also features the IMAX Discovery Theater with a screen that is six stories tall and eight stories wide. Stadium seating and 12,000-watt digital surround sound bring new meaning to the term "3-D" in this educational theater. Broadway is also home to Planet Hollywood, NASCAR Speedpark, the All-Star Café and Hard Rock Café.

Comfortably situated on the Intracoastal Waterway, Barefoot Landing is the perfect vantage point for beautiful yachts that make their way out to sea. When shoppers are ready to drop, they can take in a show at the Alabama Theatre or visit one of the world's most unique animal parks. Alligator Adventure is home to approximately 1,000 alligators and crocodiles, along with a host of exotic reptiles and birds. Hopefully, the "adventure" is the closest you will come to a live alligator or crocodile. Visitors find themselves in awe, rather than fear, of these prehistoric-looking creatures. The park includes albino alligators from Louisiana and some of the most rare species of reptile in the world. Utan, one of the world's largest crocodiles, hails from the jungles of Thailand and weighs more than 2,000 pounds. The admission price may be a little high for a larger family with a jam-packed vacation schedule, so make sure you prioritize your adventures at the beach!

Fourteen miles south of Myrtle Beach is a community that thousands of visitors grace every year, Murrells Inlet. However, the vast majority of visitors literally eat and run. It is hard to go wrong with any one of the dozens of family-friendly spots known for fresh seafood. But there is much more to the Murrells Inlet area. Do-it-yourself vacationers really get into the inlet - with their waders on - to go crabbing in its waters. Deep-sea charters also depart from this area daily. Kayaks and canoes roam the more tranquil sections, while powerboats tour less-remote channels. The businesses and homes of Murrells Inlet are a treat, but they also serve as a gateway to a different brand of beaches where sea oats and sand dunes are more prevalent than roller coasters and firecrackers.

Nearby, Brookgreen Gardens is a showplace for the sculptures of its former owner, Anna Hyatt Huntington, along with the remarkable work of 200 other artists. Named "one of the top five public gardens in the South" by Southern Living magazine, Brookgreen is a visual menagerie of more than 2,000 types of plants. Children will love the wildlife park and the "walk-in birdhouse" or aviary. The garden paths are shaped like a butterfly, and even the plants themselves are sometimes sculpted works of art. Little ones will not want to miss "The Alligator." Brookgreen has such a variety of flora, there is something beautiful to see in the arboretum and gardens any time of year. It is located 3.3 miles south of Murrells Inlet on US 17, adjacent to Huntington Beach State Park. Admission is $12 for adults and $10 for seniors (older than 65).

For families on a budget, Waccatee Zoological Farm, or Waccatee Zoo, in Socastee is an entertaining alternative to the better-publicized animal attractions. The admission fee is only $3.50 for children up to age 13, and $6 for anyone 13 or over. The owners began Waccatee Zoo simply because they wanted to raise a lion. One thing led to another and their farm opened to the public in 1988. Today, their 500-acre home is home to about 100 animal species. Local residents are still more familiar with the farm than tourists, but plenty of travelers are discovering this great opportunity to see and touch wild animals. There are three trails on site and a petting zoo. Waccatee is located at 8500 Enterprise Road between the Intracoastal Waterway and SC 707.

Berkeley, Charleston and Dorchester Counties

(For hikes #23-28: Francis Beidler Swamp National Recreation Trail, Main Trail at Cypress Gardens, I'on Village Walk, Palmetto Islands County Park, Awendaw Connector of the Palmetto Trail, James Island County Park)

Charleston is the center of this diverse three-county area and obviously holds a number of wonderful family-oriented detours. But some of the most enjoyable spots are off the beaten path and in the small towns nearby. For instance, when traveling with the whole family, a comprehensive beach resort such as Seabrook Island Resort on John's Island, East and West Beach Villages of Kiawah or the quintessential Wild Dunes on the Isle of Palms may be the ticket. Seabrook is the most rustic of the three, but there is no shortage of activity or beauty on this island, which is 45 minutes from Charleston. From Memorial Day through Labor Day, children and teenagers can easily find friends. For ages 3-11, treasure hunts, hiking and more are on the daily agenda, while teens gather in the evenings for volleyball or theme parties. Call for specifics and fees. Camp Kiawah groups children by age and explores the natural elements of Kiawah Island. Also, the Discovery Series is a free weekly program featuring storytellers and naturalists as speakers. Dive-in movies at the pool, family cookouts and other activities are also available free of charge. The summer program at Wild Dunes includes Toddler Time with morning and afternoon sessions that include tumbling, arts and crafts and Breakfast With "Barney." Older children can take part in the Wild Adventure Club with crabbing, miniature golf and more.

Motorists could barrel through Awendaw itself without realizing they passed through a town en route to a trail. But a layover of at least two hours affords a visit to the Sewee Visitor and Environmental Education Center (open Tuesday to Sunday from 9 a.m. to 5 p.m.) and a meal at The Crab Pot. Operated by the U.S. Fish and Wildlife Service and the U.S. Forest Service, the 9,000 square foot Sewee Visitor Center gives a tantalizing glimpse of the Francis Marion National Forest and Cape Romain National Wildlife Refuge, along with many of the wonders found along the Atlantic Coastal Plain. The floor of the Visitor Center is a three-dimensional map protected by a transparent covering. A short film in their state-of-the-art, 80-seat theater introduces newcomers to the sights and sounds of the wild, while a miniature museum displays surprisingly lifelike creatures. (Watch out for the alligator on the floor!) There are no fees for educational programs.

Moving on to the Crab Pot, guests will find a fine Southern style menu. The dining areas are T-shirt casual and the prices are not a concern, but the Lowcountry red rice and the crab-stuffed shrimp are five-star fabulous. The truly open-minded will go for the cinnamon-topped She Crab soup – and crave it for days afterward. At the Crab Pot, there are no reservations and there is no suggestion box. Anyone with a compliment or a creative urge is invited to express it right there on the cement block wall. The staff even lets you stand on the bar and autograph the ceiling if that idea is tempting. The rustic walls also serve as a gallery, making the juxtaposition of graffiti and photography intriguing to say the least. The Crab Pot is perfect for children, would-be artists and anyone who craves great seafood.

Beaufort & Colleton County

(For hikes #28, 29 and 30: Edisto Nature Trail, Marsh Boardwalk Trail and Sea Pines Forest Preserve)

South Carolina's oldest town, Beaufort (pronounced "Byoo-fort"), is not to be confused with the North Carolina town with the same spelling but a much different sound ("BO-fort"). Founded in 1711, this underrated seaside city is 19 miles west of Fripp Island. Although it is not the tourist draw that is Hilton Head or Myrtle Beach, Hollywood has come calling on more than one occasion, making Beaufort County the location for films such as *Something to Talk About, Forrest Gump, The Great Santini* and *The Big Chill.* Beaufort is the hometown of Pat Conroy, author of *The Prince of Tides,* which was also filmed there and on Fripp Island. It is difficult to label an area within the town of Beaufort as an historic district, but the downtown – with all of its delicacies and treasures – is just that.

Bicycles are a perfect way for families to explore Beaufort. Whether exercise or sightseeing is the goal, the town offers many opportunities. The "Tour de Frogmore" is one of many trails ranging from 20 to 40 miles long. Public boat landings are easy to find in Beaufort, a perfect launching point for discovering the Intracoastal Waterway and surrounding islands. Beaufort residents celebrate seafood every October during the annual Shrimp Festival, which features a Frogmore Stew cook-off. Those who are new to the area need not worry – the stew does not contain frogs!

For families who opt for the traditional resort fare, the Palmetto Dunes Resort on Hilton Head Island is reputed to be one of the best in the Southeast for families. With 2,000 acres of villas, homes and hotels, championship golf courses and three miles of coveted beachfront, this area is a classic for

Carolina tourists. For children ages 4-12, the Vacation Station at the Hilton is a popular spot for games and activities. Fees range from $20 to $35 per day for guests and non-guests. Babysitters are also easy to access.

Nearby Fripp Island has been listed among the "100 Best Golf Resorts in North America" by "Links" magazine, but there are 100 other reasons to visit this coastal oasis. One is Fripp Island Resort's newest attraction – the $2 million Cabana Club, which features a lagoon with secret caves and waterfalls, an alligator slide, a giant frog fountain, a heated oval pool and a bubbling spa. The resort offers activities for families, along with special programs for children and teens. Golf and tennis lessons are available for all ages. The arts and crafts program includes activities ranging from tye-dying T-shirts to creating great souvenirs from the shells you find on the beach. For the nature-minded, the staff naturalist teaches guests about native flora and fauna every Tuesday evening in the summer. From Memorial Day to Labor Day, Camp Fripp is another way to say "vacation heaven" for kids ages 5-12. Little ones may enjoy a Kid's Night Out, while teens have a Casino Night and parents dine at their leisure. The Beach Club is a top choice for a Sunday brunch, a casual dinners and an ocean view. Restaurants that cater to any mood or taste are found within the resort. From fishing supplies to poolside fashions, resort stores offer everything a vacationer could want.

Just five miles from Hunting Island State Park, St. Helena Island looks like the opening shot of many movies that depict a remote tropical paradise. The Gullah culture is prominent on this lush island where scuba divers enjoy some of the clearest waters of the South Atlantic. Visibility is often better than 20 meters. Divers are treated to the sight of many fish and underwater fauna that are unique to St Helena. The island is home to the world's most remote golf course, and sport fishing expeditions leave daily at dawn.

Island cuisine reflects the cultures that have inhabited it over the years, as opposed to the typical seafood fare of Beaufort. Curry, black pudding, pumpkin stew, fishcakes, and coconut fingers are a few samples of the exotic fare. Tuna, wahoo and mackerel are always fresh and tasty alternatives. For an interesting twist on fast food, the Shrimp Shack, located across from the shrimp docks on St. Helena Island, is known for serving the best shrimp burger in the Lowcountry.

For more information

Barefoot Landing (800) 272-2320
Berkeley County Chamber of Commerce and Visitor Bureau (800) 882-0337
Broadway at the Beach (800) 386-4662
Brookgreen Gardens (800) 849-1931
Buck Hall Recreation Area (843) 887-3257
Carolina Buggy Tours (Beaufort) (843) 525-1300
Carriage Tours of Beaufort (843) 521-1651
Charleston Area Convention and Visitors Bureau (843) 853-8000
Fripp Island Resort: (800) 845-4100
Georgetown County Chamber of Commerce (800) 777-7705
Greater Beaufort Chamber of Commerce (800) 638-3525
Greater Summerville/Dorchester Chamber of Commerce and Visitors Center (843) 873-2931
Harborwalk Festival (843) 546-1511
Hopseewee Plantation (843) 546-7891
Hunting Island State Park Phone: (843) 838-2011
Isle of Palms (800) 845-8880
Kiawah Island (800) 845-2471 in SC or (800) 654-2924 outside SC
Myrtle Beach Area Chamber of Commerce (800) 356-3016
Palmetto Dunes Resort (800) 845-6130
Pawleys Island House Tour (843) 546-5685
Pinckney Island National Wildlife Refuge (912) 652-4415
Pritchards Island Reservations (843) 575-7432
Samworth Wildlife Management Area (843) 546-9489
Seabrook Island Resort (800) 845-2475
Sewee Visitor and Environmental Education Center (843) 928-3368
The Crab Pot (843) 887-3156
The Original Hammock Shop (800) 332-3490
The Pavilion (843) 913-5200
The Woodlands Resort and Inn (843) 875-2600
Waccatee Zoological Farm (843) 650-8500

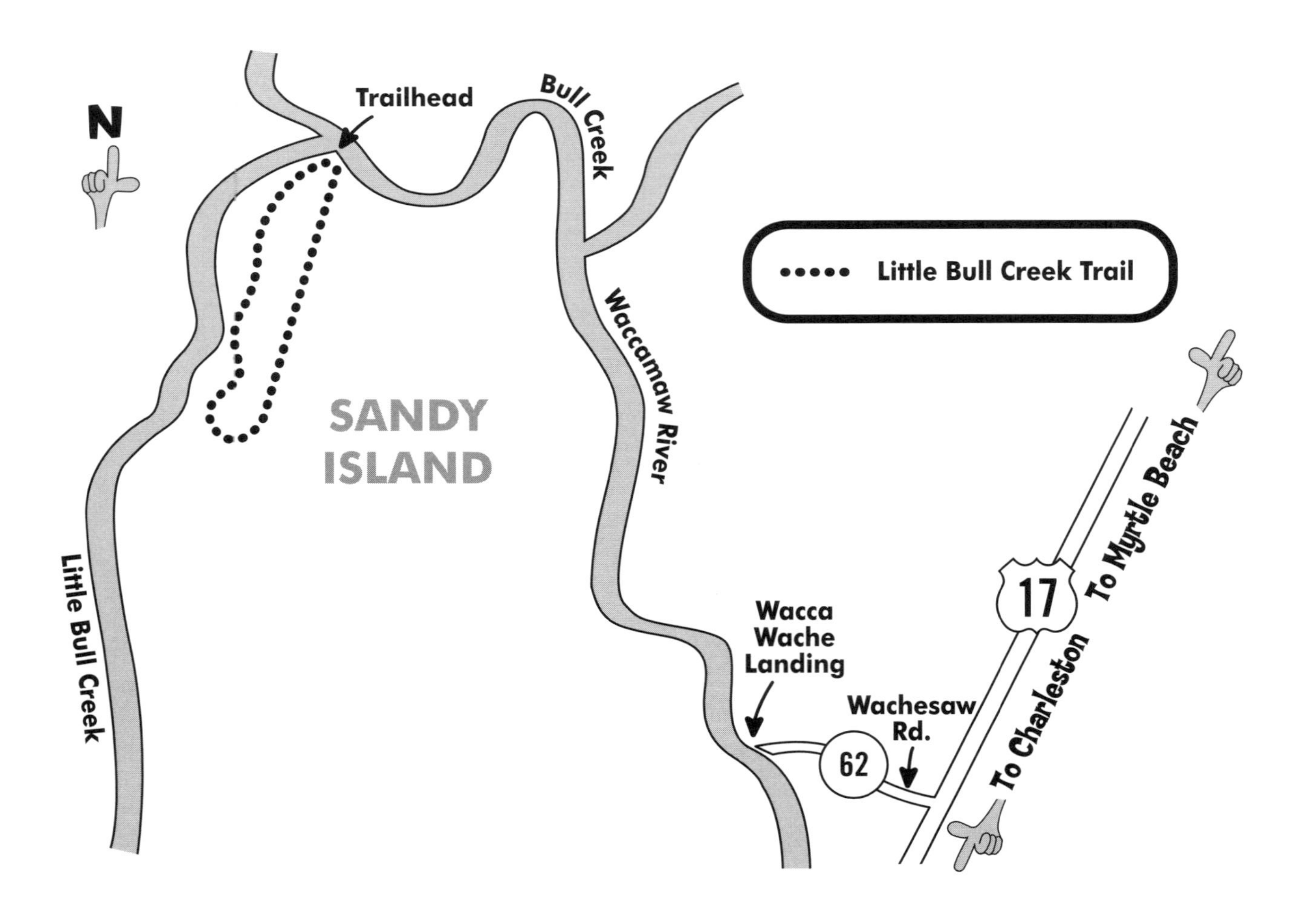
N
Trailhead
Bull Creek
Little Bull Creek Trail
Waccamaw River
SANDY ISLAND
Little Bull Creek
Wacca Wache Landing
Wachesaw Rd.
62
17
To Charleston
To Myrtle Beach

Little Bull Creek Trail

21

Location: Sandy Island, north of Pawley's Island (Georgetown County)
Directions: From Myrtle Beach, drive south on US 17 to Murrell's Inlet and turn right (west) onto Wachesaw Road. Follow about 2 miles to the upper overflow parking lot of Wacca Wache Landing (there is no parking at the landing itself). Drive time from Myrtle Beach is 30 minutes. From the landing, go north up the Waccamaw River to the first major tributary entering the Waccamaw on the left (west) side of the river. This is Big Bull Creek. Follow the creek about 1 mile to Little Bull Creek on the left. About 25 yards before Little Bull Creek, look for a small opening in the shoreline vegetation and remnants of a boat dock. Beach your boat and start exploring...
Hiking Time: About 2 hours, plus the paddle or boat trip from Wacca Wache Landing. This is the only hike in this guide that requires access by boat.
Distance: 2.5 miles
Difficulty level: Easy, although logistically difficult because of the water access.
Trail surface: Natural, mostly flat and level.
Trail markings: The trail is marked with blue blazes.
Uses: Walking, birding.
Facilities: None at Wacca Wache Landing or on the island. Boat rentals available from Black River Outdoors Center and Expeditions, (843) 546-4840 or www.blackriveroutdoors.com.
Best time to visit: Summer. Remember that biting insects are common.
Dogs: Yes
Fees: No fee to access the island or hike, but you will need to rent a boat, canoe or kayak if you do not have access.
Hours: Dawn to dusk. No camping.
For more information:
The Nature Conservancy
Winyah Bay Project Office
PO Box 1660
Georgetown, SC 29442
(843) 527-2557
www.nature.org

Family Perk

Ask local outfitters about guided kayak trips. You don't need experience and even small children can ride in tandem kayak with parents.

Photo courtesy James Luken.

Although this isolated, 9,000-acre preserve is one of the most special land forms in South Carolina, Sandy Island is not well known among hikers because it is well off the beaten path. The only access to the easy, 2.5-mile Little Bull Creek Trail is by boat. But if you can arrange a trip, this is one of the most rewarding family hikes in the guide because it has a high adventure quotient and involves a trip to a fantastic natural resource.

The Little Bull Creek Trail (and adjacent 4.5-mile Red Cockaded Woodpecker Trail) takes visitors through the red cockaded woodpecker habitat. The northern end of the island is covered by longleaf pines, many of which are more than a century old. Cypress and tupelo swampland thrive on the other side of the island where hikers will find pitcher plants and orchids. Massive dunes, including one that is 75-feet high, are an awesome sight on the island's beach. Sandy Island's creeks were once used to transport rice grains to market. Today, the 24-square-mile land mass is a wildlife haven, a historical treasure and a cultural anomaly. Visitors may see the tracks left by bobcats, black bear or whitetail deer in the sand – tracks that will thankfully leave their impressions forever.

Everyone is welcome on Sandy Island during daylight hours. However, certain activities are prohibited in order to protect the environment. The Wildlife Management Area Agreement (WMA) regulates hunting. Contact the S.C. Department of Natural Resources for specifics. The Nature Conservancy also asks that visitors be respectful of private property owners. This is easy to do by observing WMA boundary markers.

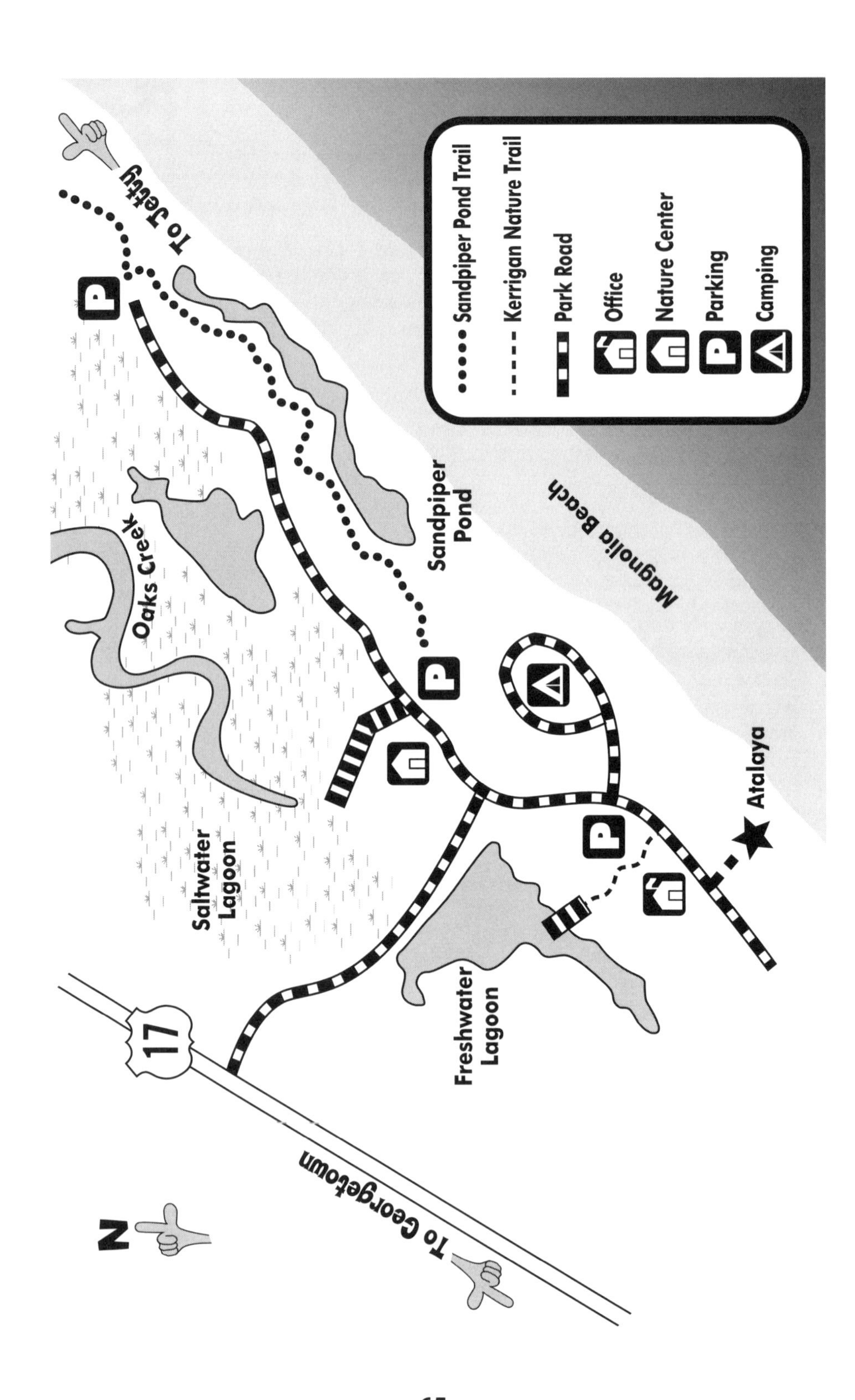

Sandpiper Pond Trail
Kerrigan Nature Trail
Park Road
Office
Nature Center
Parking
Camping
To Jetty
Sandpiper Pond
Magnolia Beach
Oaks Creek
Saltwater Lagoon
Freshwater Lagoon
Atalaya
17
To Georgetown
N

Sandpiper Pond Trail

Location: Huntington Beach State Park, near Murrell's Inlet (Georgetown County)
Directions: From Myrtle Beach, drive south on US 17 S to Murrells Inlet. Huntington Beach State Park is on the left (east), three miles south of Murrells Inlet.
Hiking Time: About 40 minutes, but allow time for birding
Distance: 2 miles (round trip)
Difficulty level: Easy
Trail surface: Dirt path, but uneven and rolling. Not good for wheelchairs or those with mobility impairments.
Trail markings: The trail is marked and easy to follow.
Uses: Walking, birding. Camping is allowed in campgrounds.
Facilities: Restrooms and water are located in the Visitors Center.
Best time to visit: Winter is by far the best time to visit for the excellent birding opportunities, but many families will be in the area during summer vacation. Bring insect repellent whenever you come.
Dogs: Yes, on a leash.
Fees: $5 per adult; $4.25 for seniors and $3 per child ages 6 to 15. It is free for children 5 and younger.
Hours: Open 6 a.m. to 6 p.m. from Saturday through Thursday and until 8 p.m. on Fridays and Saturdays. Hours are extended to 10 p.m. daily during Daylight Savings Time.
For more information:
Huntington Beach State Park
16148 Ocean Highway
Murrells Inlet, SC 29576
(843) 237-4440

Family Perk

Huntington Beach has an extensive program list with eco-activities in summer (beachcombing) and winter (birding).

One of the South's purest beaches with 2 miles of virgin coastline, the 2,500-acre Huntington Beach State Park is also arguably the finest birding location on the entire East Coast. Some would say the best way to experience this environment is via the 1-mile Sandpiper Nature Trail, a moderately easy trek from the boardwalk (wheelchair accessible) to the beach. During the two-mile round trip, travelers may spy on regal tundra swans or spot a loggerhead turtle while marveling at the dunes. Alligators skulk along the freshwater lagoon as the path weaves in and out of various habitats.

The park was named after New York sculptor Anna Hyatt Huntington and her husband Archer who built a castle-like retreat, Atalaya, on the property during the Great Depression. Atalaya, which is Spanish for watchtower, is a fortress type structure with its own 40-foot tower. Huntington's sculptures are also displayed at nearby Brookgreen Gardens.

Photo courtesy James Luken.

The park has an ample number of campsites at two separate grounds, however reservations are recommended. Each site, excluding the designated tent sites, has water and electrical hookups and is convenient to hot showers and restrooms. Some sites have sewer hookups. Several sites accommodate RVs up to 40 feet, others up to 30 feet. A dump station is available for RV users. While tent campers may use the sites with water and electricity, the park also offers a designated walk-in tent site area, which includes tent pads and central water. The primitive group camping area is suitable for organized groups of up to 200 people. The area includes picnic tables, a fire ring and nearby restroom facilities.

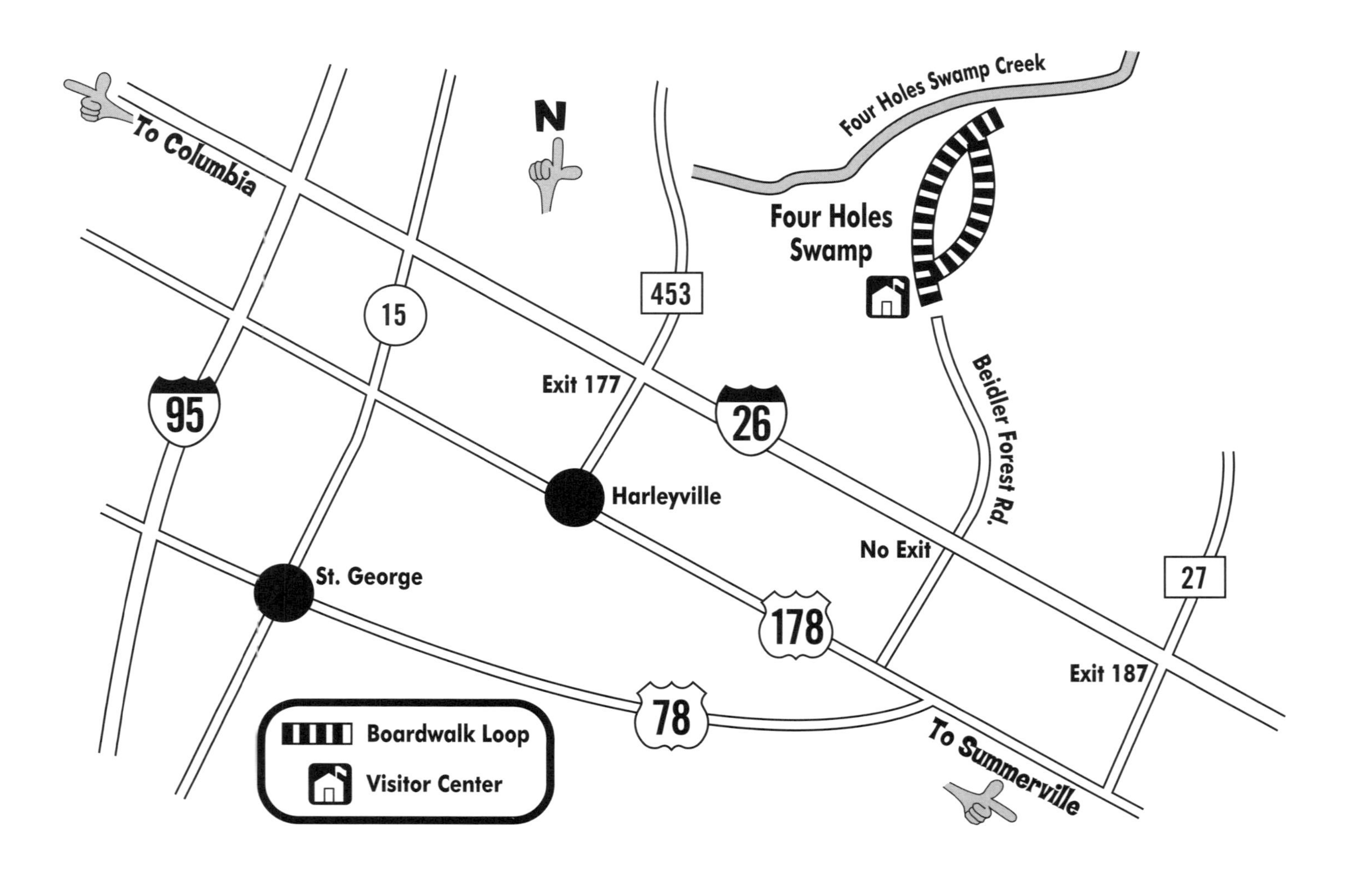

Four Holes Swamp Creek
Four Holes Swamp
Beidler Forest Rd.
N
To Columbia
453
15
Exit 177
26
95
Harleyville
No Exit
27
St. George
178
Exit 187
78
Boardwalk Loop
Visitor Center
To Summerville

Audobon Center at Francis Beidler Forest

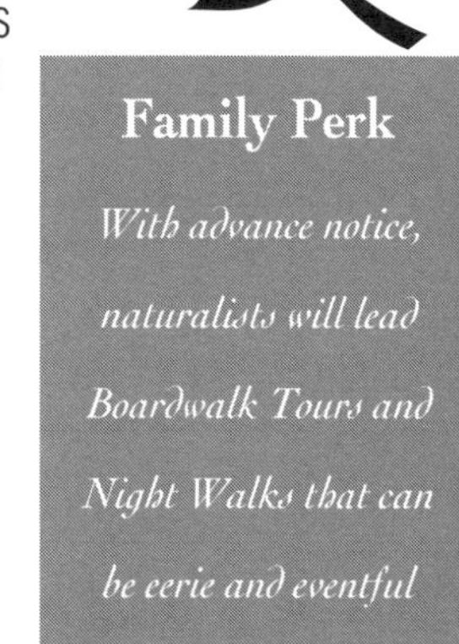

Location: Audobon Center at Francis Beidler Forest near Harleyville (Dorchester County)
Directions: From Charleston, take Interstate 26 west to exit 187. Turn left (south) onto SC 27 and follow to US 78. Turn right (west) and, at the fork, bear right onto US 178. Follow to a right turn onto Francis Beidler Forest Road, which is the first paved right. Follow "Beidler Forest" signs five miles to the forest.
Hiking Time: Around 1.5 hours (round-trip)
Distance: Nearly a 2-mile loop
Difficulty level: Easy
Trail surface: Wooden boardwalk.
Trail markings: None, you shouldn't have trouble following the boardwalk.
Uses: Walking, birding, educational activities. No camping.
Facilities: Restrooms and gift shop located in the visitor's center. The forest also has a conference room, outdoor classroom and Meeting Tree. All facilities are accessible for the mobility impaired.
Best time to visit: Fall is an excellent time at the forest because it is one of the most colorful places in the Lowcountry. Spring is excellent for bird watching.
Dogs: No
Fees: $6 per adult ($5 for Audubon, Nature Conservancy or AAA members); $3 per child ages 6 to 18. Children 5 and under are free.
Hours: Open Tuesday through Sunday from 9 a.m. to 5 p.m. Closed on most holidays.
For more information:
Francis Beidler Forest
336 Sanctuary Road
Harleyville, SC 29448
(843) 462-2150
www.beidlerforest.com

Photo courtesy Leigh Ann Kornegay.

It's a rare instance that one trail, a 1.75-mile boardwalk (incidentially one of the longest in the state), could have such great appeal to families from all over the country. Yet every year, many families drive off a main highway and into backwater South Carolina to spend several hours staring up into the surrounding forest. But the Audobon Center at Francis Beidler Forest is not your everyday forest either. In fact, it's the largest remaining virgin stand of tupelo gum and bald cypress trees in the world. The canopy can grow to a height of 120 feet and the entire Francis Beidler Forest is almost 13,000 acres. The forest is actually part of the larger (40,000-acre) Four Holes Swamp, which stretches 60 miles across four different counties. For perspective, the entire swamp is almost as large as Lake Murray near Columbia.

The forest's raison d'etre is to protect the mammoth, 1,500-year-old trees, many of which tower over the trail in awe-inspiring fashion. It is managed by the National Audubon Society, which also provides staff at the visitor's center, which serves as the gateway to the entire sanctuary. The center was built on a raised foundation to allow free passage of swamp water below and inside you can find brochures and a numbered guide to the boardwalk, which has a rain shelter and short spur to Lake Goodson for more expansive views. Children may especially enjoy the chance to view wildlife through binoculars and it's a good idea to visit in the morning hours when there are fewer people and quiet conditions.

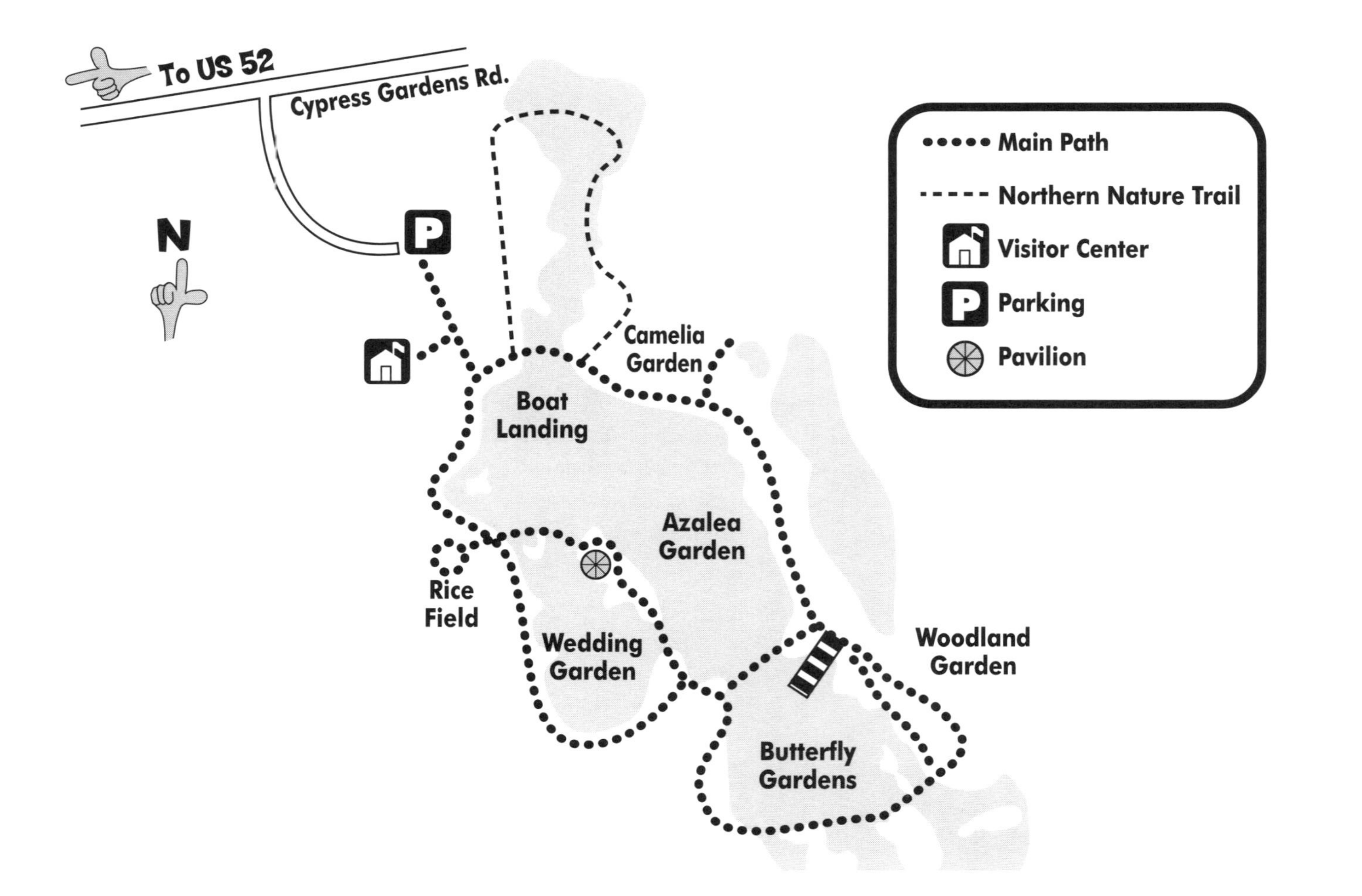
To US 52
Cypress Gardens Rd.
N
Main Path
Northern Nature Trail
Visitor Center
Parking
Pavilion
Camelia Garden
Boat Landing
Azalea Garden
Rice Field
Wedding Garden
Woodland Garden
Butterfly Gardens

Main Trail, Cypress Gardens

24

Location: Cypress Gardens near Moncks Corner (Berkeley County)
Directions: From Charleston, follow Interstate 26 west to exit 208 for US 52W toward Goose Creek. Follow US 52 to a right onto Cypress Gardens Road. Continue through a flashing light and follow to the end of Cypress Gardens Road to the entrance.
Hiking Time: Two hours
Distance: Loops of 0.75 to 1 mile (The gardens features over 4 miles of trails.)
Difficulty level: Easy
Trail surface: The trails are mainly on old dikes from plantation days. Surfaces include manicured garden paths and boardwalks.
Trail markings: The main path is well-marked, the more remote trails are not quite as easy to follow.
Uses: Walking, picnics, wildlife viewing and birding.
Facilities: Restrooms, water and picnic areas are located near the gift shop at the front entrance. No camping.
Best time to visit: Spring is best to enjoy blooming narcissus, daffodils, camelias and azaleas but popular events take place in the fall including Halloween in the Swamp.
Dogs: Yes, on a leash.
Fees: $9 per adult; $8 for 65 and older and $3 per child ages 6 to 12. Children 5 and under are free. Group rates apply for 15 or more. Fees include all activities in the gardens, including boat rental. Free parking.
Hours: Open daily 9 a.m. to 5 p.m. Closed on some major holidays.
For more information:
Cypress Gardens
3030 Cypress Gardens Road
Moncks Corner, SC 29461
(843) 553-0515
www.cypressgardens.info

Family Perk

Children will love the Butterfly House but rent a bateau (flat-bottomed boat) and paddle a marked route through the swamp.

Photo courtesy Oliver Buckles.

Although Cypress Gardens is tucked away in South Carolina's coastal plain 40 minutes from the tourist spots in downtown Charleston, this county-owned 250-acre garden is a must-visit for families looking for a great walking trip and natural experience. The Cypress Gardens has an excellent walking system of flat, easy trails with the popular 0.75 to 1 mile interconnecting loops of the Main Path as the centerpiece through and around a black water swamp. And while taking a self-guided tour (walking brochures are available) can help parents explain the plants and animals you'll see along the way, you might most enjoy a bateau (flat-bottomed boat) trip to paddle the marked route through the swamp. Each boat holds between six and eight people and life jackets are available. Sorry no dogs in the boats.

The trails of Cypress Gardens range from the more accommodating Main Path circuit to the narrow, adventurous Perimeter Trail, which takes off from the Southern Nature Trail and dives into a remote swamp surrounded by rhododendron and wildlife such as alligators and egrets, white ibis and wood storks. An alligator pond also connects to a 24,000-gallon fresh water aquarium where you can see snapping turtles.

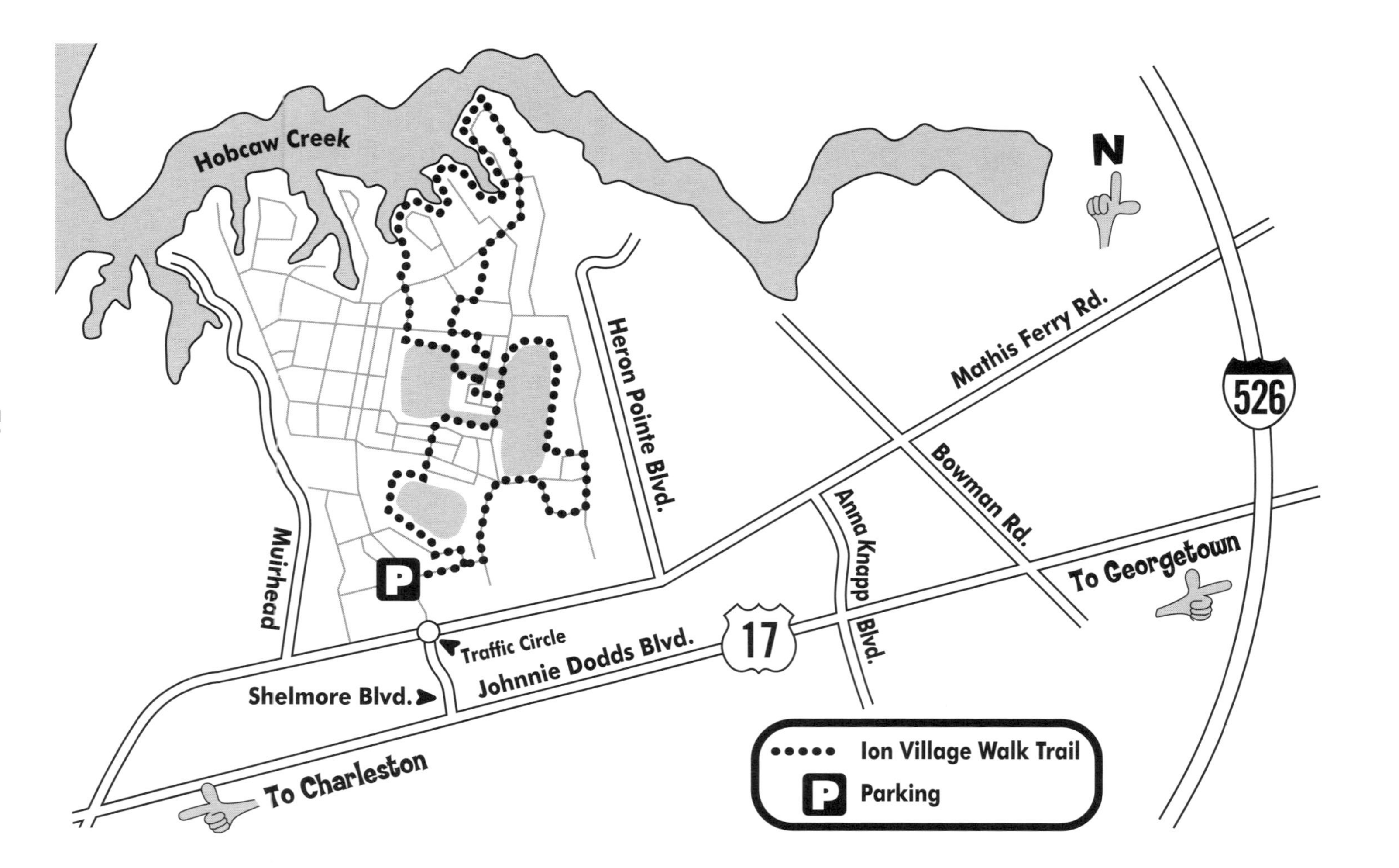
Hobcaw Creek
N
526
Mathis Ferry Rd.
Heron Pointe Blvd.
Bowman Rd.
Anna Knapp Blvd.
To Georgetown
Muirhead
P
Traffic Circle
Johnnie Dodds Blvd.
17
Shelmore Blvd.
To Charleston
Ion Village Walk Trail
P Parking

I'on Village Walk

Location: I'On Village, Mount Pleasant (Charleston County)
Directions: From Charleston, follow US 17 east to Mount Pleasant. Turn left onto Shelmore Boulevard. Pass through the traffic circle and continue to the square. Park behind the building at 10 Resolute Lane.
Hiking Time: About 2.5 to 3 hours
Distance: 5-mile loop (1.8-mile and 3.2-mile options are also possible
Difficulty level: Easy
Trail surface: Natural, mostly flat and level. Mostly wheelchair accessible; loops exist to circumvent some steps.
Trail markings: No, but the route is very easy to follow. For additional help, download the online I'On Village Walk guide.
Uses: Walking, birding. Camping is not allowed.
Facilities: Bathrooms are available at several downtown establishments. There is also a coffee shop and pub nearby. There are also many spots for picnics along the way.
Best time to visit: Late fall, winter and early spring are best. Biting insects are common in warm weather.
Dogs: No, there are alligators in the Rookery.
Fees: None
Hours: Dawn to dusk
For more information:
I'On Village Walk
10 Resolute Lane
Mount Pleasant, SC 29464
(843) 216-2646
www.ioncommunity.com

Family Perk

Families, Cub Scouts, schools or church groups can earn an I'On Village Walk patch for completing the entire walk and answering educational questions.

Photo courtesy William Hamilton.

There are other fine examples of urban trails in South Carolina such as greenways that connect schools, libraries, athletic clubs and communities. But the easy, 5-mile I'On Village Walk provides an extraordinary glimpse into how new urbanist developments can combine environmental, historical and architectural features into one community and serve as both a great resource for residents and visitors alike. While you can enjoy views of the Rookery Wildlife Refuge and other wildlife, it is best to approach this outing not as a hike but as an enlightening tour of a painstakingly designed village with a palpable sense of history and architecture.

Volunteers designed the Village Walk as a self-guided tour of some of the more interesting features within the 256-acre I'On community in Mount Pleasant. The route begins at a triangular grass island in the center of the square and follows sidewalks into the community, gaining trails into and around the Rookery Wildlife Refuge. The Village Walk will take visitors into different ecosystems and along different types of walking paths that show off many interesting architectural features of the homes and bridges throughout the village. A free downloadable Internet guide (see Web site address above) provides many additional details about the area. (The guide is also available for $5 from many of the businesses on I'On Square; fees help cover the project cost and go into the Mount Pleasant Green Space Fund.)

If you cannot walk the entire 5-mile loop, it is easy to shorten the hike to a 1.8-mile or 3.2 mile loop walk.

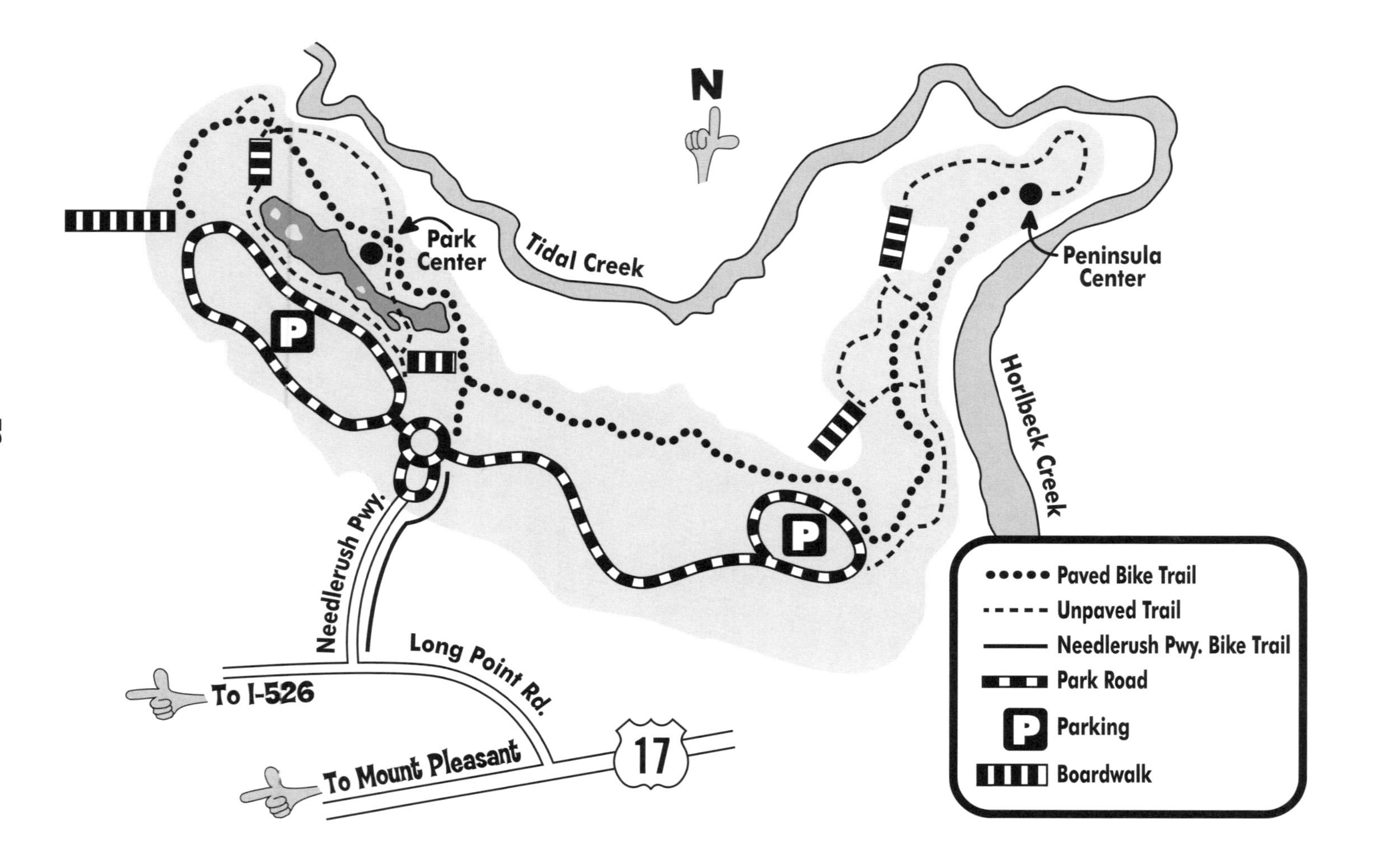
N
Park Center
Tidal Creek
Peninsula Center
Horlbeck Creek
P
Needlerush Pwy.
Long Point Rd.
To I-526
To Mount Pleasant
17
Paved Bike Trail
Unpaved Trail
Needlerush Pwy. Bike Trail
Park Road
Parking
Boardwalk

Palmetto Islands County Park

26

Location: Palmetto Islands County Park (Charleston County)
Directions: From North Charleston and Interstate 526, drive to the Long Point Road Exit, turn left (east). Drive 2.1 miles and turn left at the park sign onto Needlerush Parkway. Drive 1.2 miles to the end of the road and park entrance. From Mount Pleasant, follow US 17 North to a left turn onto Long Point Road at a sign for Boone Hall Plantation. Continue to a right turn at Needlerush Parkway.
Hiking Time: 30 minutes to 2 hours
Distance: 4.6 miles of interconnecting trails
Difficulty level: Easy
Trail surface: Some paved trails, boardwalks and spots of sandy footpath.
Trail markings: Yes, trails are signed and blazed.
Uses: Walking, biking, picnics, fishing. Splash Island Waterpark is open in summer.
Facilities: Restrooms, beverages, snacks and bike rentals are available at the Park Center.
Best time to visit: Spring and fall. Summer is the only time to enjoy the Waterpark.
Dogs: Yes, on a leash.
Fees: $1 per person (ages 2 and younger are free)
Hours: 9 a.m. to 6 p.m. in March, April, September and October; 9 a.m. to 7 p.m. in May through August; 10 a.m. to 5 p.m. in November through February.
For more information:
Charleston County Parks
James Island County Park
871 Riverland Drive
Charleston, SC 29412
(843) 884-0832
www.ccprc.com

Family Perk

With a 200-foot slide, recreational pool, otter slides and more, the Splash Island Water Park is a must-visit destination in summer. Call ahead for admission rates.

Although you will find the usual kid-oriented amenities such as Splash Island Waterpark and numerous picnic shelters, Palmetto Island County Park is far more nature-oriented than the swanky James Island County Park on the other side of Charleston. But the 4.6-mile trail network is tailor made for a family trip and even picky hikers will be able to choose between paved trails or sandy footpaths through tidal marshes. The trails are all easy to follow and some include self-guided interpretive sections while a 50-foot observation tower affords great views of Horlbeck Creek and the surround wetlands.

One of the best trails in the park is the Nature Island Trail, a 1.2-mile footpath that crosses a boardwalk to an island and continues through a series of wetlands. The trail is surrounded by a lush, tropical forest of palmetto oak, magnolia and cedar and crosses a tidal creek where birding is a popular pastime. Visitors can pick up a trail brochure in the park to learn about plants and trees along the trail. Although it is very short, the 0.2-mile Osprey Trail leaves from the park center and offers great walks for very young children or toddlers because it ends at a boardwalk with stunning views of the creek and some nearby osprey nests.

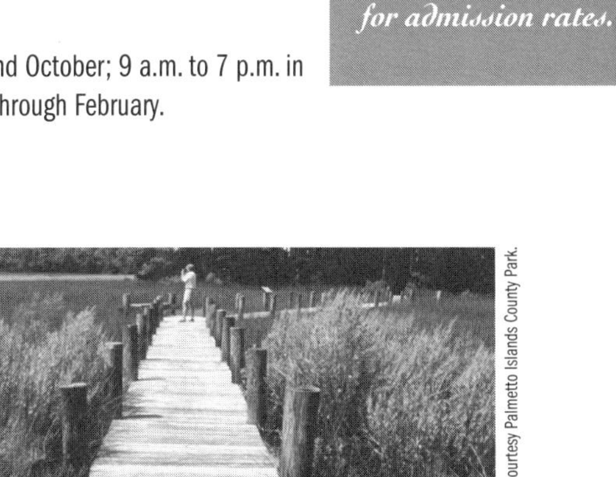

Photo courtesy Palmetto Islands County Park.

Two paved bikes trails crisscross the peninsula and help connect all the other trails in the park. These trails are really just a leg-stretcher for adults but children will enjoy the terrain, distance and scenery along the way.

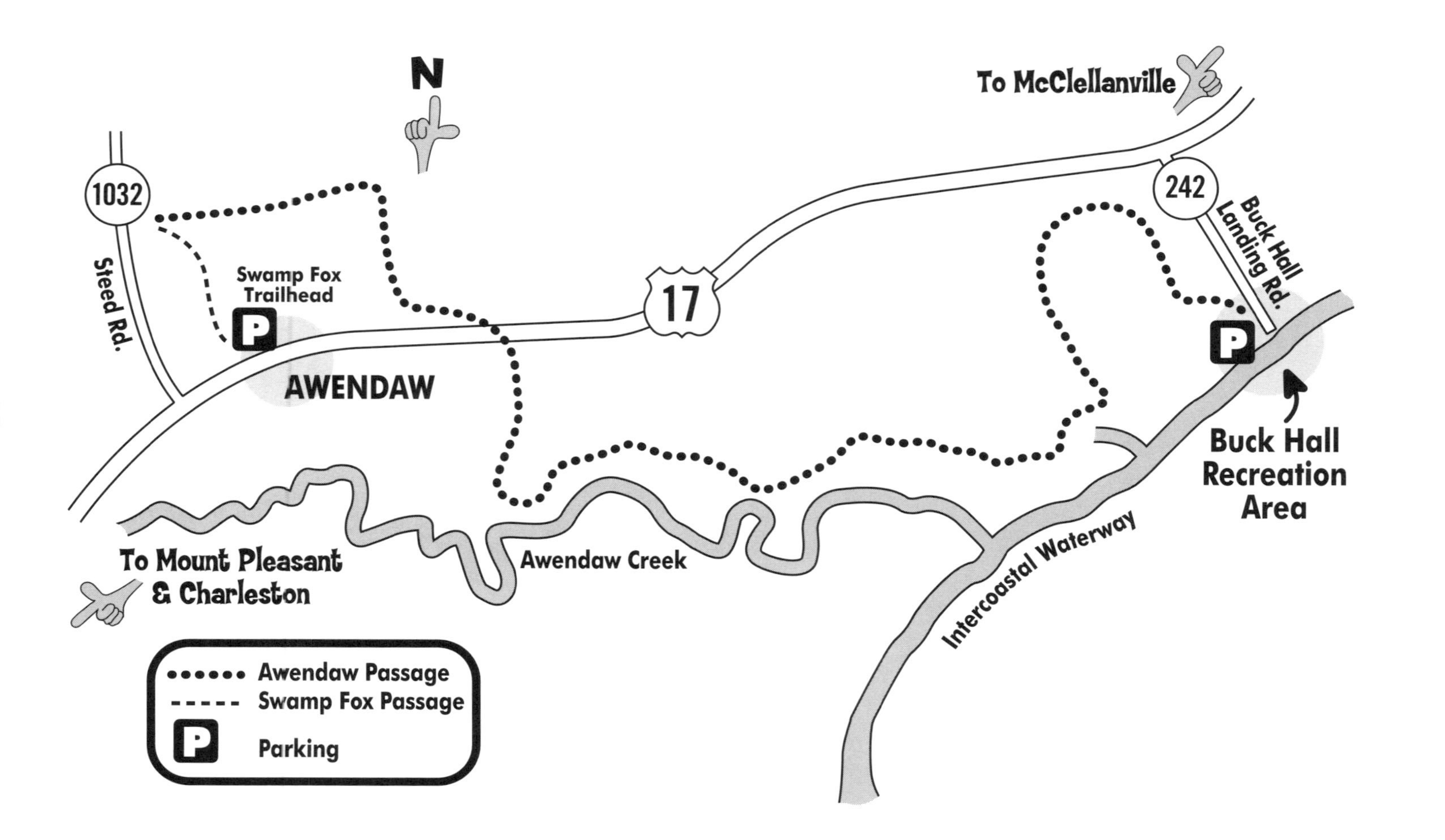

N
To McClellanville
1032
Steed Rd.
Swamp Fox Trailhead
AWENDAW
17
242
Buck Hall Landing Rd.
Buck Hall Recreation Area
To Mount Pleasant & Charleston
Awendaw Creek
Intercoastal Waterway
Awendaw Passage
Swamp Fox Passage
Parking

Awendaw Connector of the Palmetto Trail

Location: Buck Hall Recreation Area, Francis Marion National Forest (Charleston County)
Directions: From Charleston, take US 17 north to Buck Hall Landing Road (FS 242). Turn right to access the Recreation Area. It is about 30 minutes north of Charleston.
Hiking Time: About 3 hours (one way)
Distance: 7 miles
Difficulty level: Easy
Trail surface: Natural surface (marshy and grassy) and boardwalks
Trail markings: Kiosk at trailhead. Palmetto trail blazes on route.
Uses: Hiking and mountain biking. Camping is permitted; contact the National Forest office for permits.
Facilities: Yes, restrooms and water are located near the campground.
Best time to visit: This trail is best during the late fall and winter. During temperate months, be prepared for biting insects and high temperatures.
Dogs: Yes, on a leash.
Fees: $5 parking fee to access Buck Hall Recreation Area.
Hours: Open 7 a.m. to 7 p.m. from Sunday through Thursday; 7 a.m. to 9 p.m. on Friday and Saturday. Closing hours extended during Daylight Savings Time.
For more information:
Sewee Visitor and Environmental Center
5821 Hwy. 17 N.
Awendaw, SC 29429
(843) 928-3368

Family Perk

The nearby Sewee Visitor and Environmental Education Center is an amazing resource. Ask about the live red wolf display, live bird programs, young explorer series and more.

Photo courtesy Tom Savage.

The Awendaw Connector of the Palmetto Trail extends the planned 425-mile Mountains to Sea Trail route to its southernmost terminus: the Intercoastal Waterway. But families will enjoy this easy, 7-mile trail that starts from the Buck Hall Recreation Area in McClellanville because it offers a fantastic trip through shaded passages of live oak and across tidal creeks with views of marshes and the Intracoastal Waterway.

Ironically, until this trail opened in March 2002, there were actually no palmetto trees on the Palmetto Trail. South Carolina's famous state tree itself is restricted to a belt of maritime forest, growing right behind the tidal creeks and barrier dunes of the Atlantic coast, amid live oaks and laurel oaks. But as soon as this passage opened, the Palmetto Trail earned its name, penetrating a beautiful maritime forest as the 7-mile "seaward leg" of this ambitious cross-state path.

Not only does it have palmetto trees, but also live oaks and longleaf pines and sturdy bridges and a varied topography. The trail features incredible views of the salt marsh and tidal creeks that make the South Carolina coast a beautiful mosaic of colors and textures. For about three miles, the trail runs along the edge of Awendaw Creek on high firm ground, often climbing up to bluffs that are as much as 30 feet above the tidal creek surface. Near the confluence of the creek and the Intracoastal Waterway, the trail passes through the old Walnut Grove Plantation property, where a side trail leads through an avenue of live oaks and continues to US 17 for an alternate start or finish. The Buck Hall terminus of the trail offers secure parking, restrooms, camping and picnicking. A small day-use fee allows the Francis Marion National Forest to keep Buck Hall clean and safe.

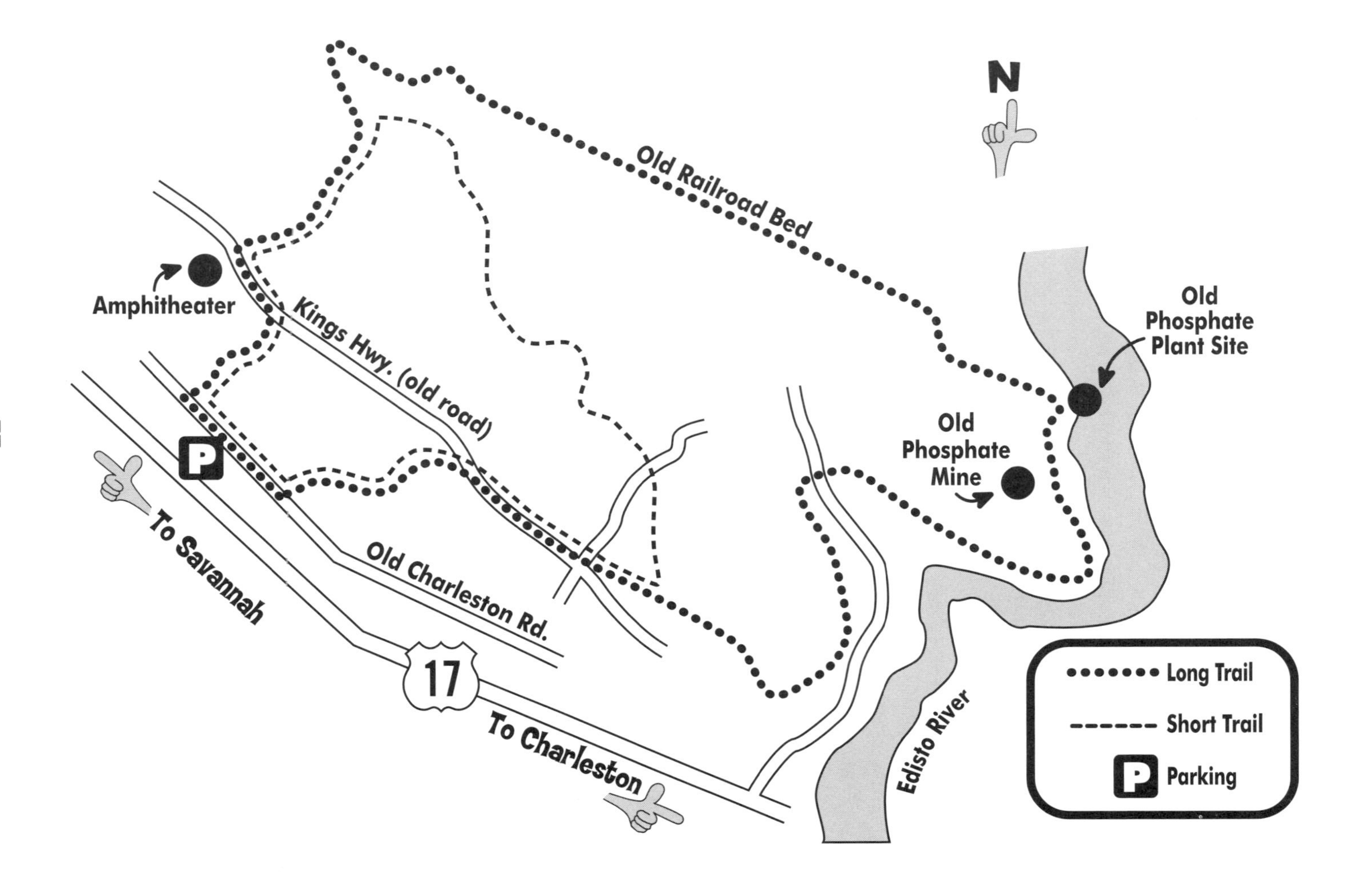
N
Old Railroad Bed
Amphitheater
Kings Hwy. (old road)
Old Phosphate Plant Site
Old Phosphate Mine
Old Charleston Rd.
To Savannah
17
To Charleston
Edisto River
Long Trail
Short Trail
P Parking

Edisto Nature Trail

Location: ACE Basin Gateway, MeadWestvaco (Colleton County)
Directions: From Charleston, follow US 17 north 31 miles toward Beaufort. The Edisto Nature Trail trailhead is on the right (north) side of the highway. You can't miss the large (lighted) wooden sign, but you will see it just after a bridge over the Edisto River and immediately before two convenience stores in the town of Jacksonboro.
Hiking Time: 1 hour
Distance: 1.5 miles in two loops
Difficulty level: Easy
Trail surface: Natural surface trails are hard-packed sand under a dense forest. Trails can be wet and raised wooden causeways allow access across boggy spots.
Trail markings: The trail includes interpretive wooden markers; grab a brochure from the mailbox at the trailhead.
Uses: Walking, nature study, birding and wildlife viewing.
Facilities: None at the trailhead. There are two convenience stores nearby and full-service camping is available at nearby Colleton or Edisto State Parks.
Best time to visit: Summer is most popular since many families vacation at nearby Edisto, Kiawah or in the Beaufort area. Late fall and winter is pretty and quiet.
Dogs: Yes, on a leash.
Fees: None
Hours: Dawn to dusk.
For more information:
MeadWestvaco
Timberlands Division
PO Box 1950
Summerville, SC 29484
(843) 871-5000
www.meadwestvaco.com

Family Perk

The trail brochures in a mailbox just inside the trailhead are packed with educational information about the forest and its wildlife.

Photo courtesy Oliver Buckles.

In every part of the state, there are "granddaddy" trails - ones that have been around so long they almost blend into the countryside. The easy, 1.5-mile Edisto Nature Trail is one of those trails. Opened to the public in 1976 and designated a Community Millennium Trail by the White House Millennium Council in 2000, the trail is owned and managed by the paper and packing manufacturer MeadWestvaco, which has extensive timberlands in South Carolina. The company uses this trail to demonstrate how working forests can produce timber while also providing wildlife habitat, clear air and water.

The Edisto Nature Trail doesn't offer exciting amenities like water parks or environmental centers, instead allowing this typical Lowcountry forest to show off its "natural" state. With more than 63 species of plants and trees (many of them labeled) this is a great opportunity to learn new plants or how to avoid others such as poison ivy (!). In the fall, the forest is awash in reds (blackgum and sweetgum) and yellows (sycamore and poplar) while in spring the trail passes flowering dogwood and yellow jessamine.

One of the best things about the trail is how the interpretive stations explain the different points of interest, including transition zones, an old phosphate mine, and rice field dikes. The "long" trail features wonderful views of the Edisto River swamp, eventually gains an old railroad bed and follows a portion of the old King's Highway - a stagecoach road that once connected Savannah with Charleston. According to the trail brochure available at the parking area, George Washington even traveled the road in 1791.

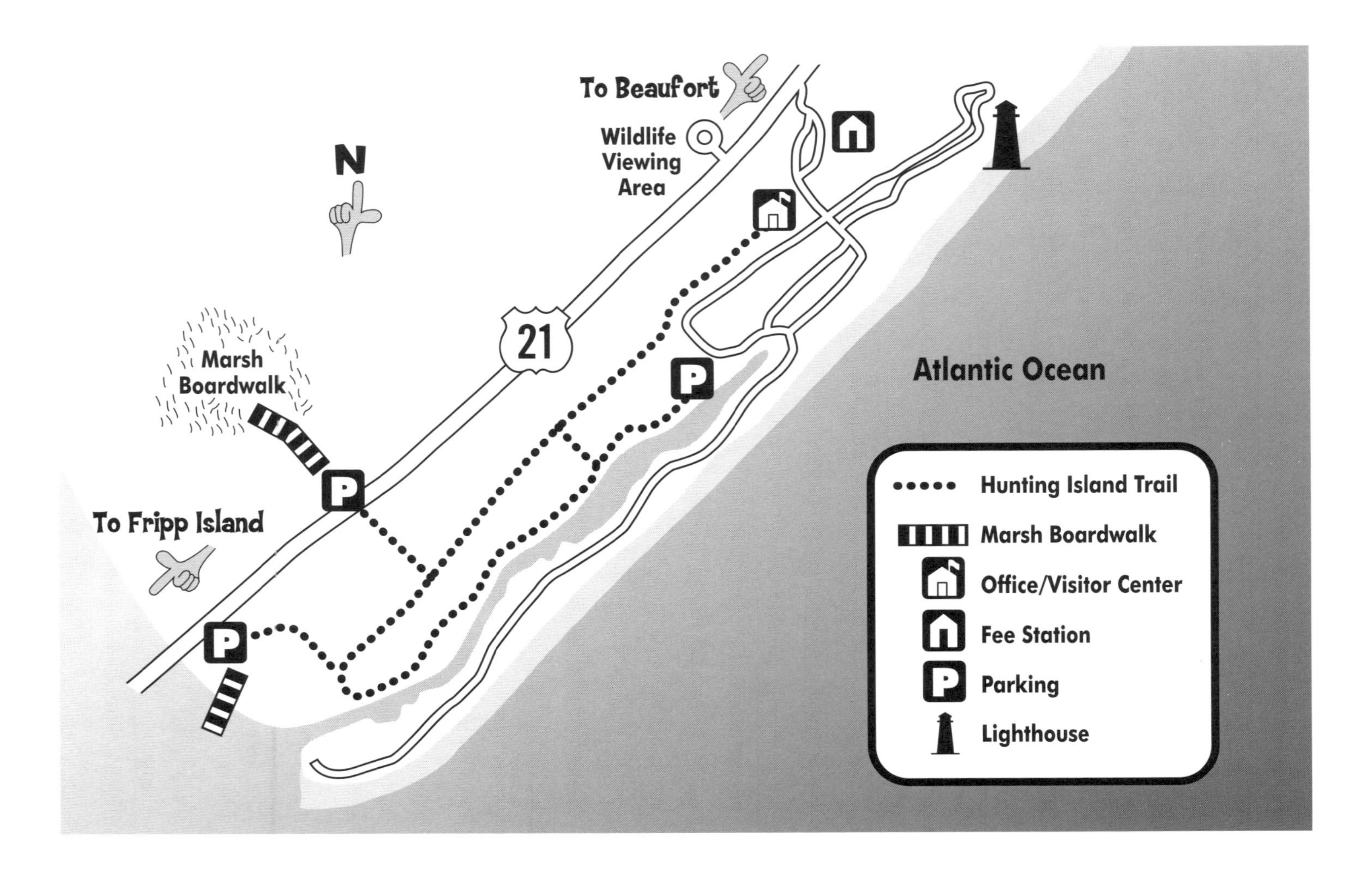

To Beaufort
Wildlife Viewing Area
N
21
Marsh Boardwalk
To Fripp Island
Atlantic Ocean
Hunting Island Trail
Marsh Boardwalk
Office/Visitor Center
Fee Station
Parking
Lighthouse

Marsh Boardwalk Trail

Location: Hunting Island State Park (Beaufort County)
Directions: From Beaufort, drive east on US 21, following signs to the park entrance on the left (Turn left here onto Hunting Island Drive to reach the Visitors Center and Park Office for maps. There is a $3 fee to enter the park). For the Marsh Boardwalk Trail trailhead, continue on SC 21 approximately 1.5 miles to a dirt parking lot on the right. There is no fee to use this trail.
Hiking Time: About 1 hour
Distance: 0.5 miles (one way)
Difficulty level: Easy
Trail surface: The first part of this trail is an aging wooden boardwalk. Follow this 1,300 feet to several small islands on a gorgeous sandy path. The boardwalk is good for those with mobility impairments but it does not have handrails.
Trail markings: The boardwalk is not blazed, but it is easy to follow.
Uses: Walking, birding, fishing. Camping is allowed in campgrounds. Mountain biking is allowed on the Lighthouse Nature Trail and on the beach.
Facilities: Restrooms and water are located at the North Beach near the lighthouse and also in the campground
Best time to visit: Summer. The beach at Hunting Island is one of the prettiest anywhere.
Dogs: Yes, on a leash.
Fees: $3 per adult; $2.50 for seniors and free for ages 15 and younger.
Hours: Open 6 a.m. to 6 p.m. from Saturday through Thursday and until 8 p.m. on Friday and Saturday. Hours are extended to 10 p.m. daily during Daylight Savings Time.
For more information:
Hunting Island State Park
255 Sea Island Parkway
Hunting Island, SC, 29920
(843) 838-2011

Family Perk

Numerous park programs including "Secrets of the Salt Marsh" on the Marsh Boardwalk Trail offer educational opportunities for families.

Photo courtesy PCF.

Bordered by the Atlantic Ocean and St. Helena Sound, Hunting Island is South Carolina busiest state park (more than 1 million visitors annually), a 5,000-acre barrier island and semi-tropical haven that one must visit to truly appreciate. It is arguably the premiere beach park in the state and families can find any number of enjoyable experiences here – including the easy, 0.5-mile Marsh Boardwalk Trail.

The trail is certainly an attraction unto itself (more on it later) but Hunting Island has so many other opportunities for outdoor recreation it is difficult to catalog. Most importantly, perhaps, 4 miles of undeveloped beach offers some of the most varied and well-preserved shells in the South. It is the longest public beach in the Lowcountry. And while the beach is unforgettable, an 1873 lighthouse actually serves as the focal point of the park. Those who challenge the 181-step climb thrill to the awesome view, but the lighthouse has been moved twice due to the threat posed by erosion. The Lighthouse Nature Trail (0.4 miles) is one of many ways to traverse the island. Visitors should ask about a two-mile passage that leads to a lagoon where elusive wildlife can be observed and photographed. Guided sea turtle walks also are available. Reservations are recommended for the oceanside campground, which is open throughout the year. Other than relaxation, sea kayaking is likely to be the favorite activity in this area. The park's lagoon is perfect for beginners, while the more seasoned outdoorsmen will try Fripp Inlet, and of course, the Atlantic itself.

The Marsh Boardwalk Trail is accessible from a parking area on the west side of the island, far from the hubbub of the beach, lighthouse and Visitors Center. On a recent summertime trip, it was teeming with families enjoying views of the salt marsh and ambling onto the nearby islands with towering pines, live oaks and palmettos. Although you will have to make reservations in advance, park naturalists often schedule programs on the boardwalk where they will let visitors in on the secrets of one of the most productive ecosystems in the world.

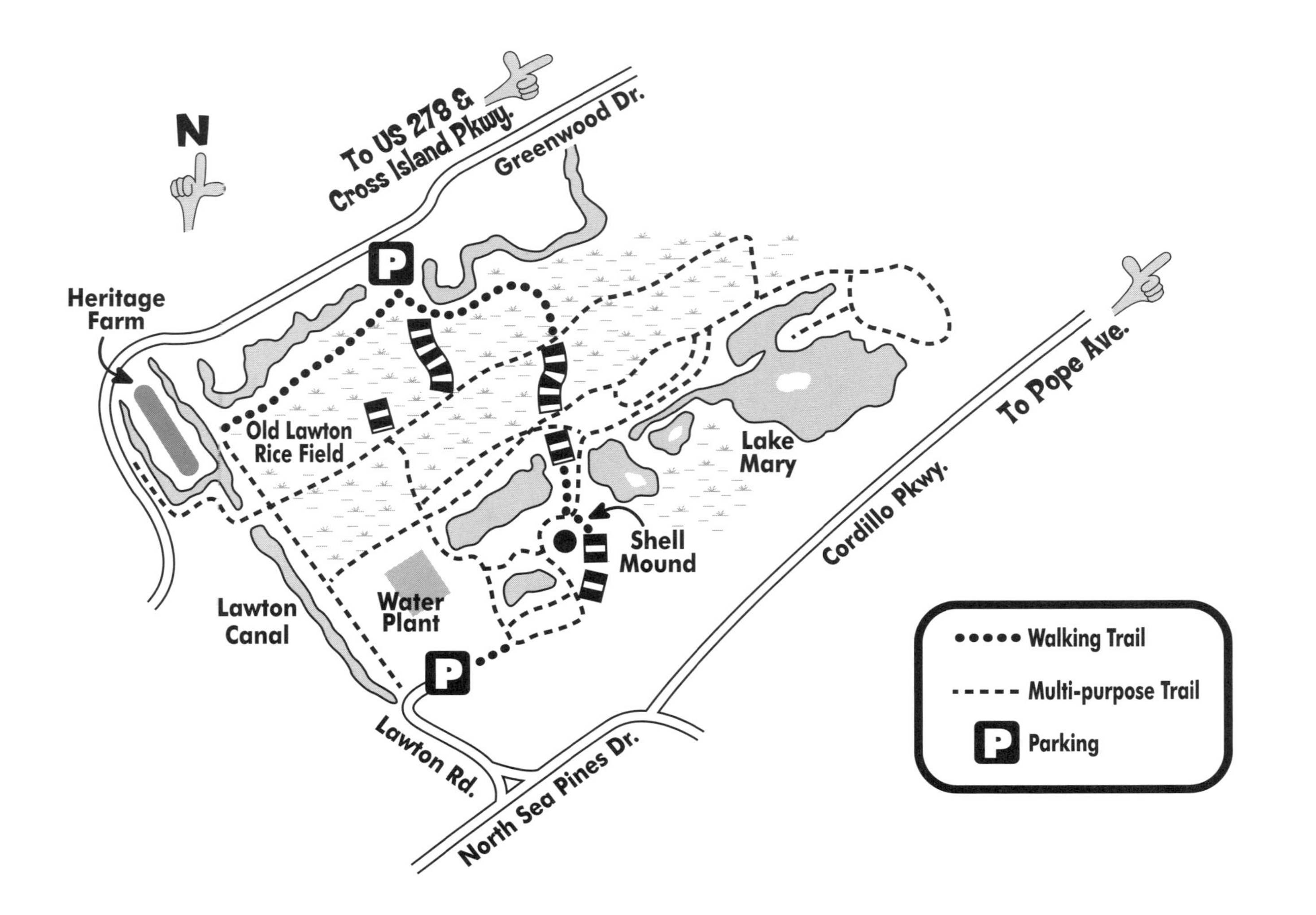
N
To US 278 &
Cross Island Pkwy.
Greenwood Dr.
Heritage Farm
P
Old Lawton Rice Field
Lake Mary
To Pope Ave.
Cordillo Pkwy.
Shell Mound
Water Plant
Lawton Canal
P
Lawton Rd.
North Sea Pines Dr.
Walking Trail
Multi-purpose Trail
P Parking

Orange Trail, Sea Pines Forest Preserve

Location: Sea Pines Forest Preserve (Hilton Head Island, Beaufort County)
Directions: From US 278 headed to Hilton Head Island, follow US 278 until you can veer left onto the Cross Island Parkway ($1 toll). Continue 4 miles to the traffic circle on Palmetto Bay Road and turn right onto Greenwood Drive. Follow to the Sea Pines gate at 0.2 mile (day use fee) and continue 0.75-mile to the preserve on the left.
Hiking Time: 30 minutes to 2 hours
Distance: 2-mile loop (the preserve has nearly 6 miles of interconnecting trails)
Difficulty level: Easy
Trail surface: A combination of paved, natural surface and boardwalk trails. Persons with mobility impairments should carefully choose a route suited to their abilities.
Trail markings: All trails are marked and blazed but the two most popular are blazed Orange (2 hour) or Blue (1 hour). Kiosks near each trailhead stocked with maps make it easy to creating your own route.
Uses: Hiking, biking, birding, fishing, and picnicking
Facilities: Restrooms, drinking water, and a picnic area are available at Fish Island, found in the center of the preserve.
Best time to visit: Summer. Numerous activities ranging from kayaking to hayrides are offered throughout the season.
Dogs: Yes, on a leash.
Fees: $5 per car and $1 per bicycle to enter Sea Pines. There is no fee at the trailhead.
Hours: Dawn to dusk. Sea Pines day-use passes are good 7:30 a.m. to 10 p.m.
For more information:
Sea Pines Forest Preserve
Sea Pines Recreation Dept.
175 Greenwood Drive
Hilton Head Island, SC
(843) 363-4530
www.csaadmin.com/forest_preserve.htm

Family Perk

Be sure to check into the preserve's fee-based "eco" trips including horseback tours, hayrides, bicycle tours, fishing and crabbing. A new favorite is the Alligator Adventure Boat Tour. Call the preserve for details.

Photo courtesy PCF.

With tranquil lagoons, well-blazed trails, salt marshes, tidal creeks, a rookery and "eco-tours" galore, Sea Pines Forest Preserve is perhaps the best "private" nature park in the Low-country. It's private in that there is a fee to enter Sea Pines Resort but the Preserve (which is just inside the gates) does an extraordinary amount of public outreach and education programs. Any visitor will feel welcome here - especially on the popular 2-mile Orange Trail.

The 605-acre Sea Pines Forest Preserve has been a protected site on Hilton Head Island since 1959 when the Fraser family, who founded Sea Pines Resort, set aside the area for wildlife habitat and outdoor recreation. (As one would suspect, humans have used it much longer. Nomadic Indians hunted and gathered shells here thousands of years ago and a 4,000-year old shell mound is a highlight of the preserve.) The first trails were installed in the 1970s and the property has been seeing incremental improvements ever since. Now, it is a favorite of locals from the Hilton Head and Beaufort areas as well as the 1.5 million resort visitors.

The entire Preserve has more than 6 miles of trails and three parking areas, but the most popular entranceway is a shady trailhead off Greenwood Road. From here, an asphalt path leads visitors to an intersection where you can choose to follow a rice dike, wooden boardwalk or natural surface trail. The Orange Trail continues across the boardwalk and leads out to an observation deck and other trails. Fish Island is at the center of the Preserve and has a picnic area with water and bathrooms available.

For history gurus the Preserve features the remnants of both a Native American village and 18th century mansion. In addition, families are sure to love the nearly 4,000-year-old shell ring composed of oysters, clams and mussel shells, together with the bones of deer, raccoons, bears, fish. This monument is nearly 150 feet in diameter and is guaranteed to capture your children's interest ... at least momentarily

Appendix

STOP! Before you go outdoors - especially with youngsters - one of the most important things you can do is familiarize yourself with the kinds of plants and wildlife you may encounter on the trail. While a complete discussion of South Carolina's flora and fauna is beyond the scope of this book, we have included a note about one particular nuisance...poison ivy.

About Poison Ivy

According to the American Academy of Dermatology, poison ivy is among the most common causes of allergic reactions in the United States. If your children spend time in the outdoors with you, you can be certain they will encounter poison ivy at some point. (Eastern poison oak is also a concern, but it is less frequent.)

Poison ivy grows in the southeast primarily as a vine. While the old saying "leaves three... let it be" is a good truism, it is also incomplete. A more exact truism would be, "leaflets of three, let it be" but also remember that lobes can have from 7 to 13 leaflets. It is important to remember that poison ivy takes on many shapes, colors and forms. Poison ivy grows as both a vine and shrub; in fall, it can turn yellow or red when other plants are still green.

If you or your children get into poison ivy, make sure you wash the exposed area with cold water. Also, wash your clothing. If a rash occurs, it is helpful to apply over-the-counter medications like calamine lotion.

Some of the photographs below may help you recognize poison ivy in common conditions found across South Carolina. All the photos below are courtesy of www.poison-ivy.org.

Index

About PCF Press

PCF Press is the publishing imprint of Palmetto Conservation Foundation, which is a South Carolina-based nonprofit, membership organization with offices in Columbia, Spartanburg and Moncks Corner. We work on projects and policy initiatives to conserve open spaces, preserve historic landmarks and promote active living, especially via trails and greenways. Learn more from our website at www.palmettoconservation.org

Also, from PCF Press...

The Waterfalls of South Carolina
This unique guide is an essential exploring companion for every resident or visitor to South Carolina's spectacular mountains. 80 pages, full color photographs and maps. Paperback $12.95.

Turtle Tracks
A girl vacationing at the beach meets a volunteer who is helping newly hatched turtle reach the water safely. Hardcover. 32 pages, full color illustrations. $12.95.

The Catawba River Companion
"The only guide to the entire Catawba River in North and South Carolina." The Charlotte Observer. Paperback. 110 pages, full color photographs and maps. $9.95.

Donny Wilder's Editor's Notebook
A "best-of" compilation of columns from Donny Wilder, the longtime editor of The Clinton Chronicle. Politics to puppy paternity, government to goats, Donny has seemingly written about every facet of small town life in South Carolina. Paperback. $9.95